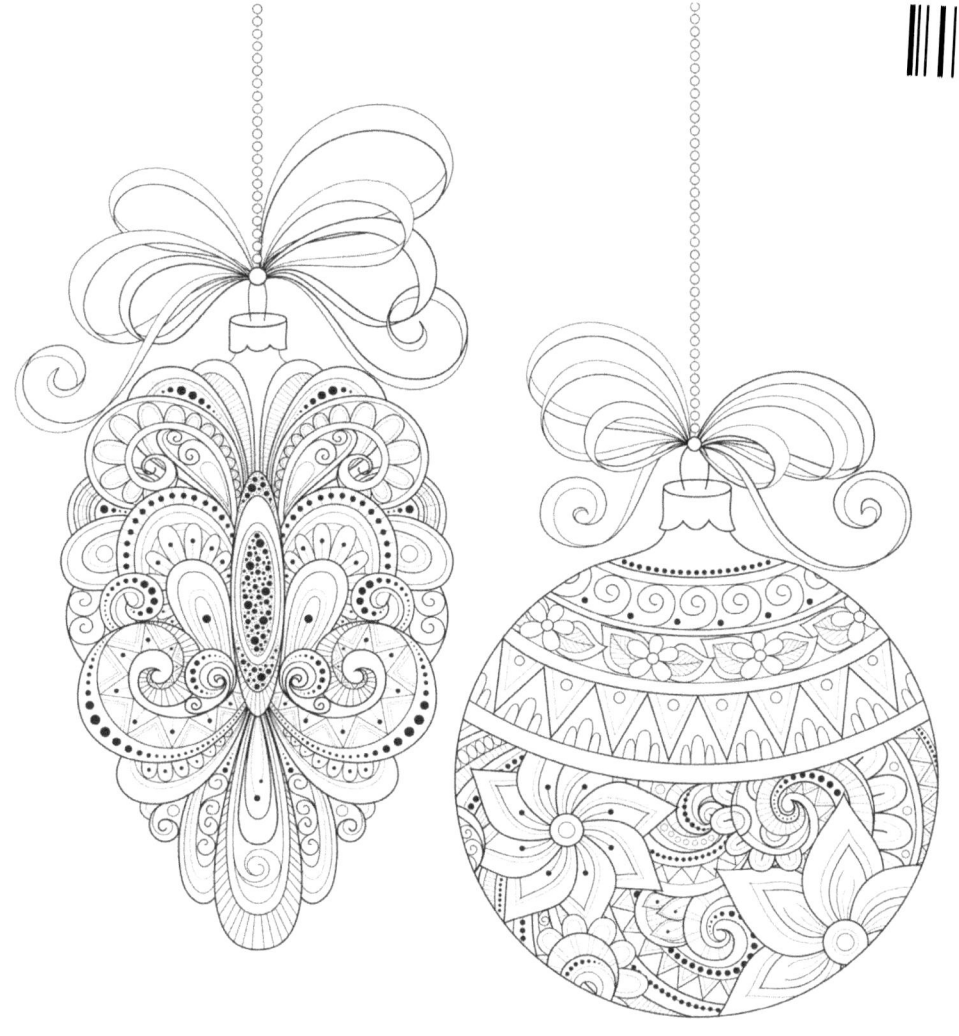

CHRISTMAS

ZENTANGLES & MANDALAS

Various Artists
Curated by Samantha West

This first installment of Samantha West's series for the experienced colorist is comprised of cheerful designs in a collection of expertly rendered coloring pages. Thirty-five beautiful and whimsical illustrations featuring zentangles and mandalas. Bring them to life with your personal coloring style for hours of relaxation and entertainment. The single-sided pages allow you to experiment with different media and makes displaying your finished creations a breeze.

International Standard Book Number
ISBN-13: 978-1539882206
ISBN-10: 1539882209

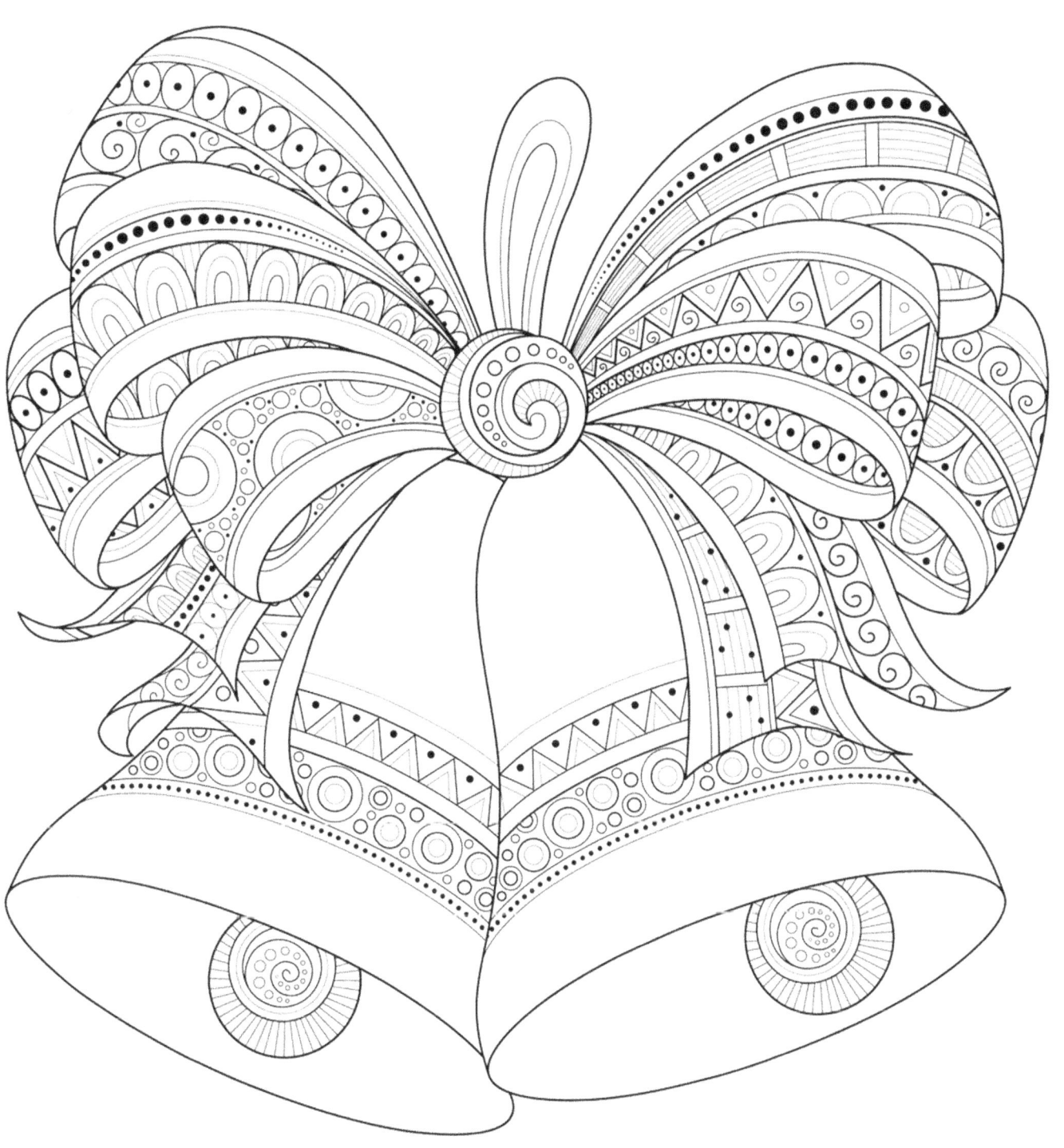

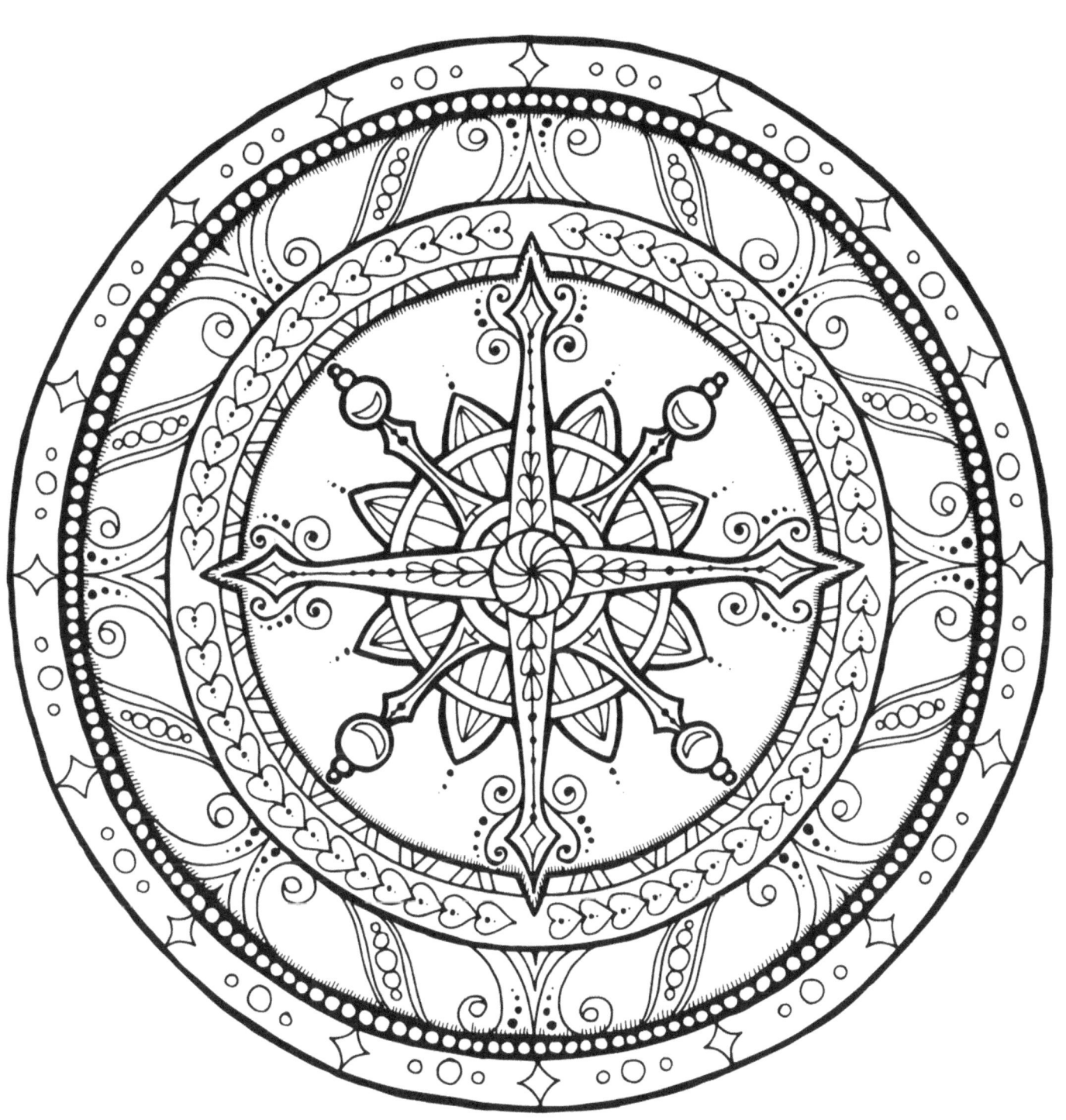

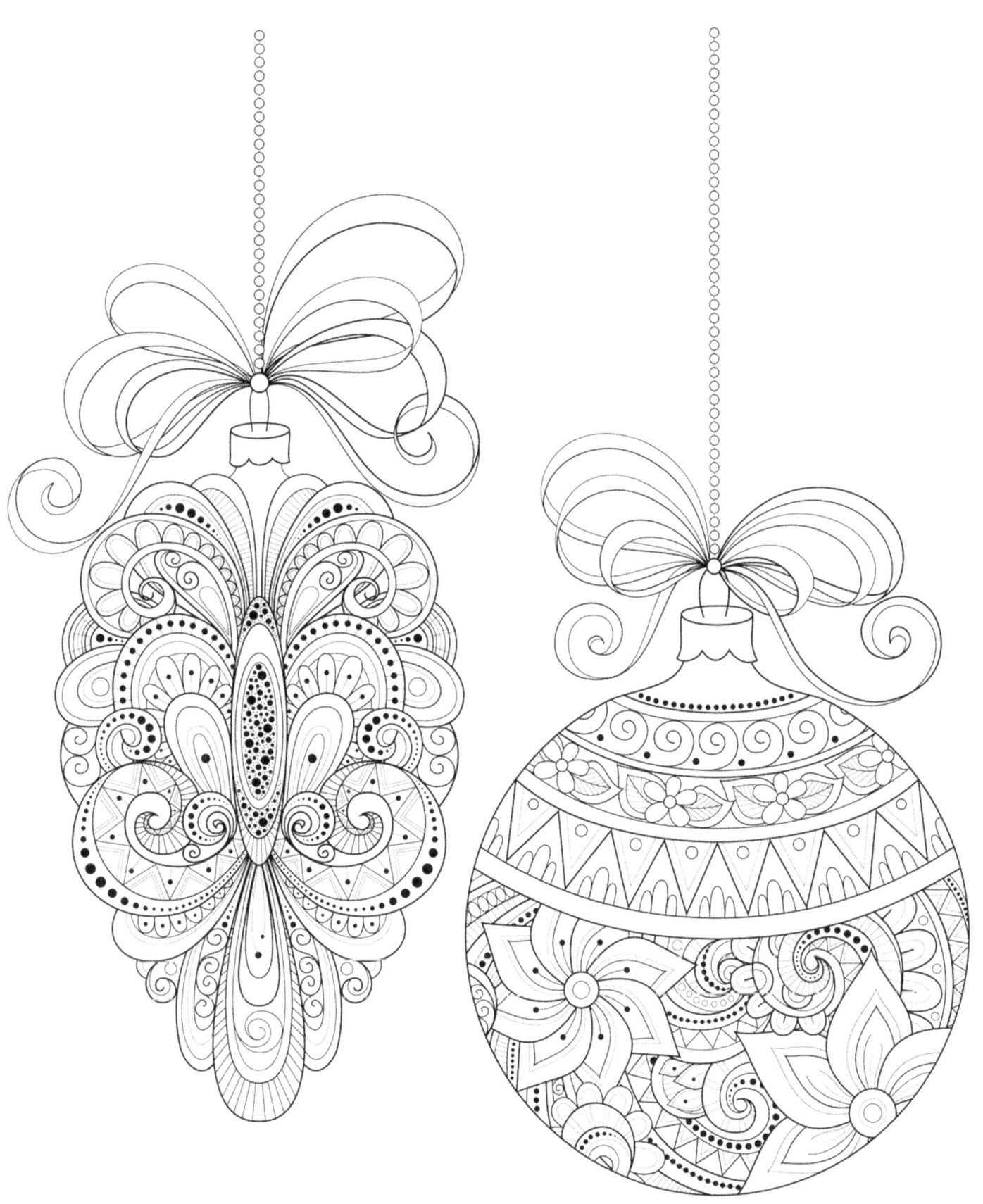

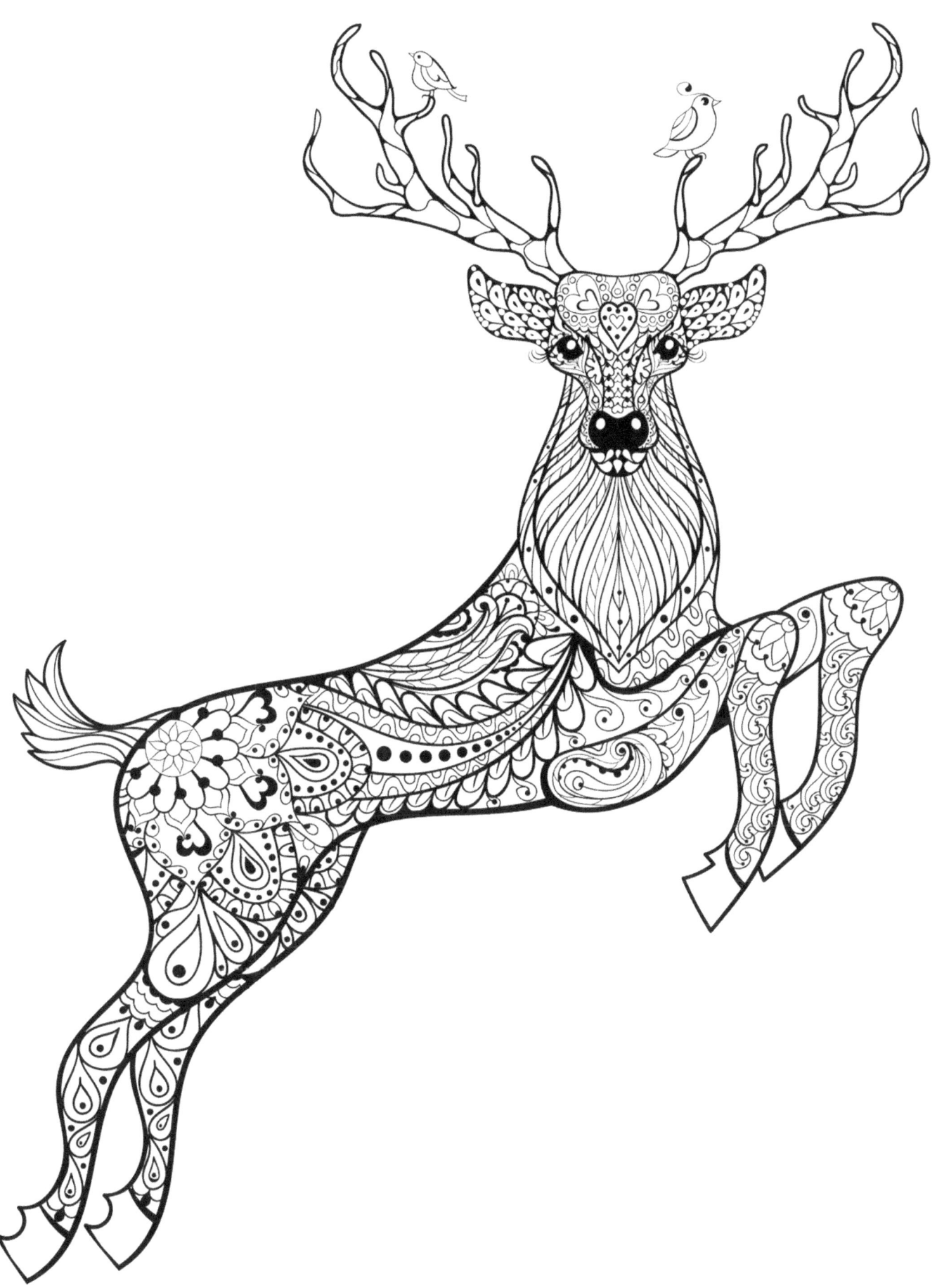

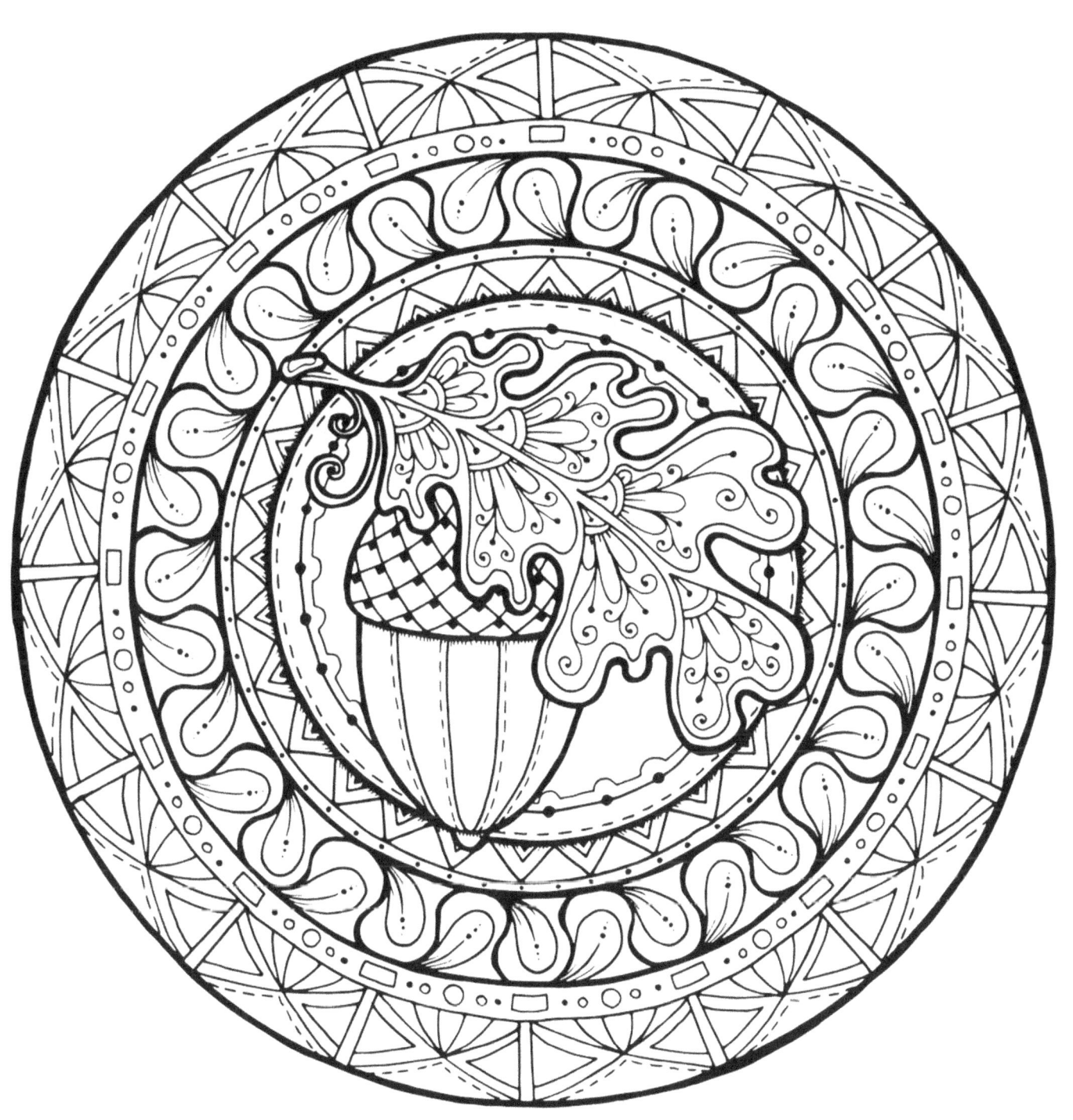

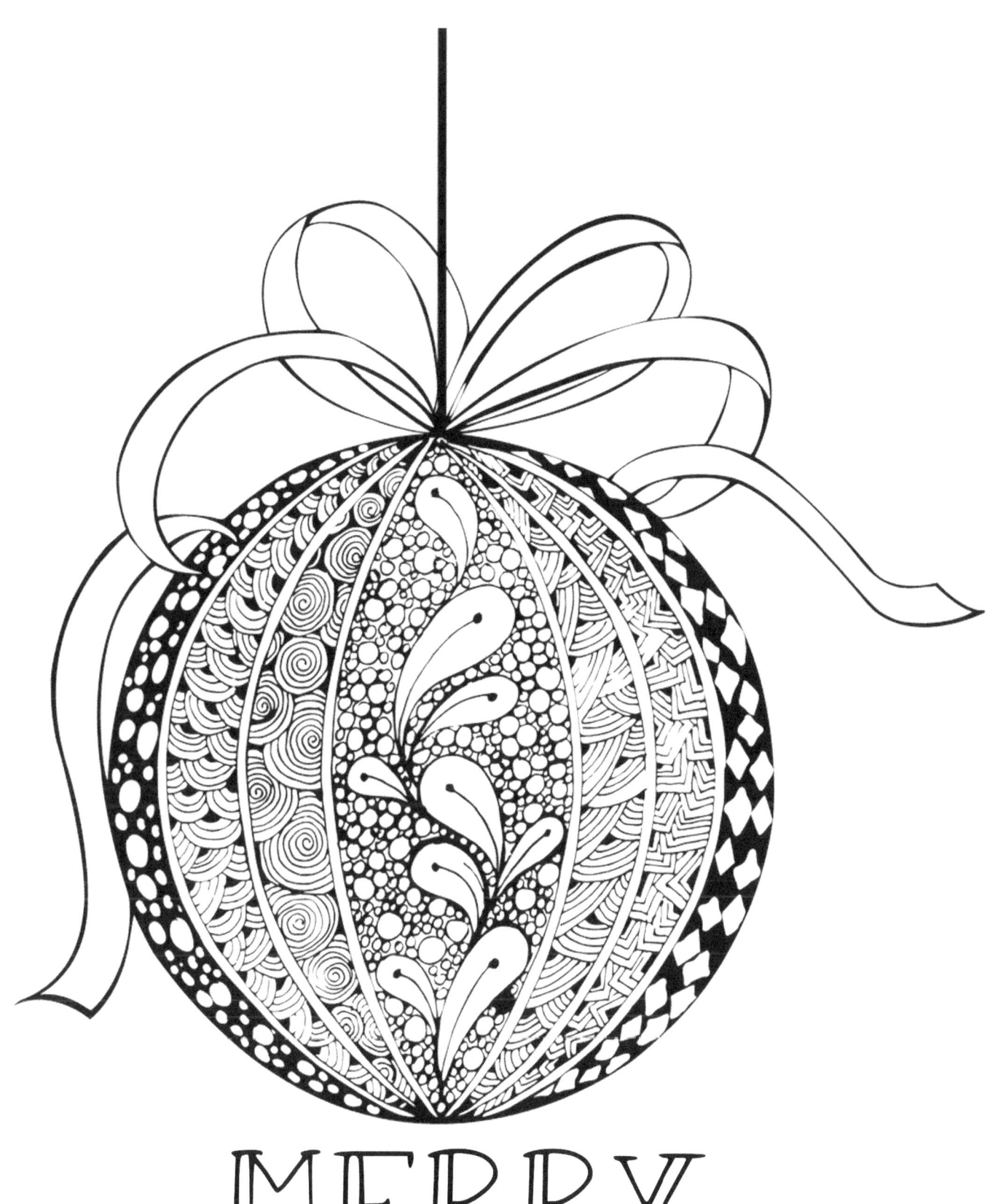

MERRY

CHRISTMAS

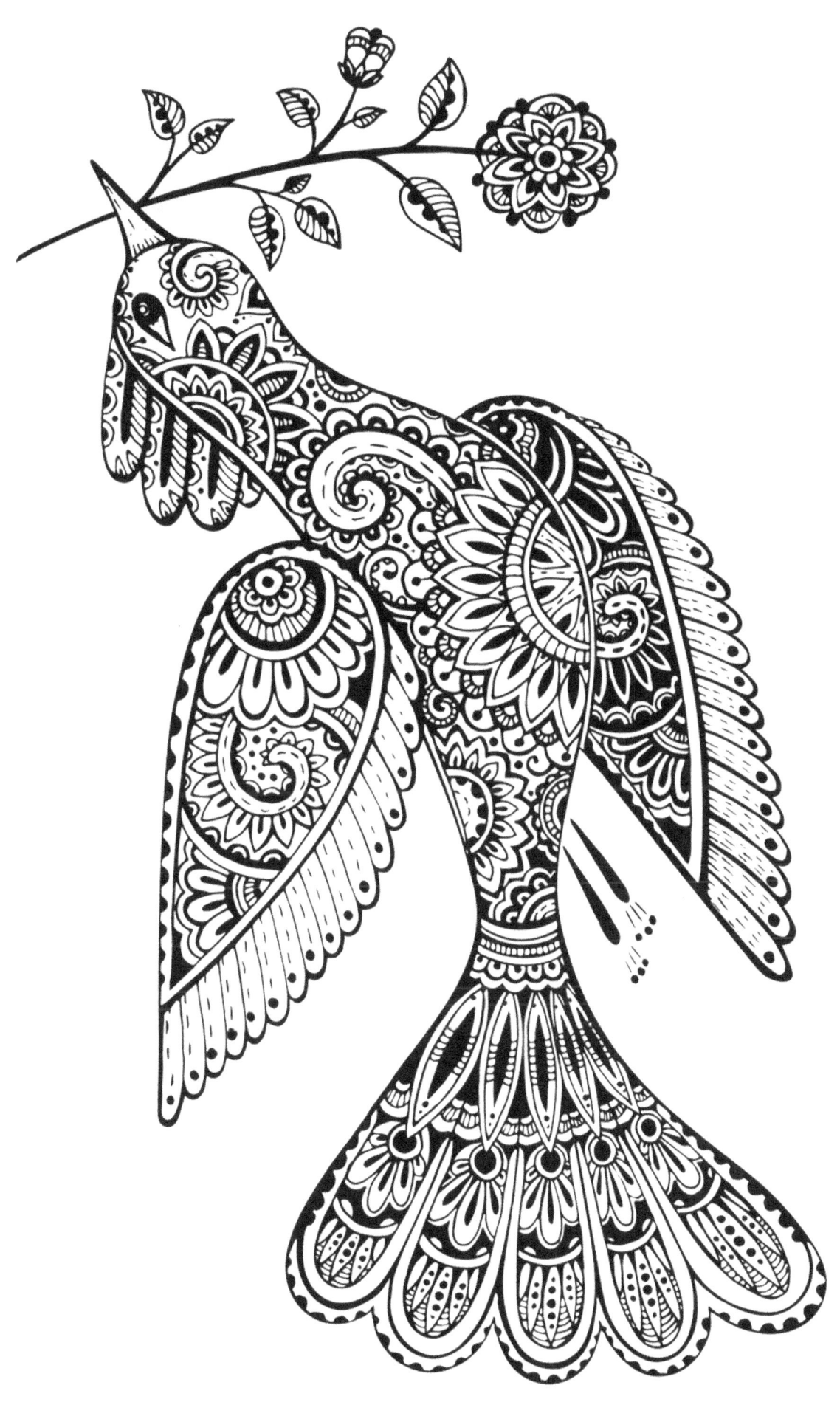

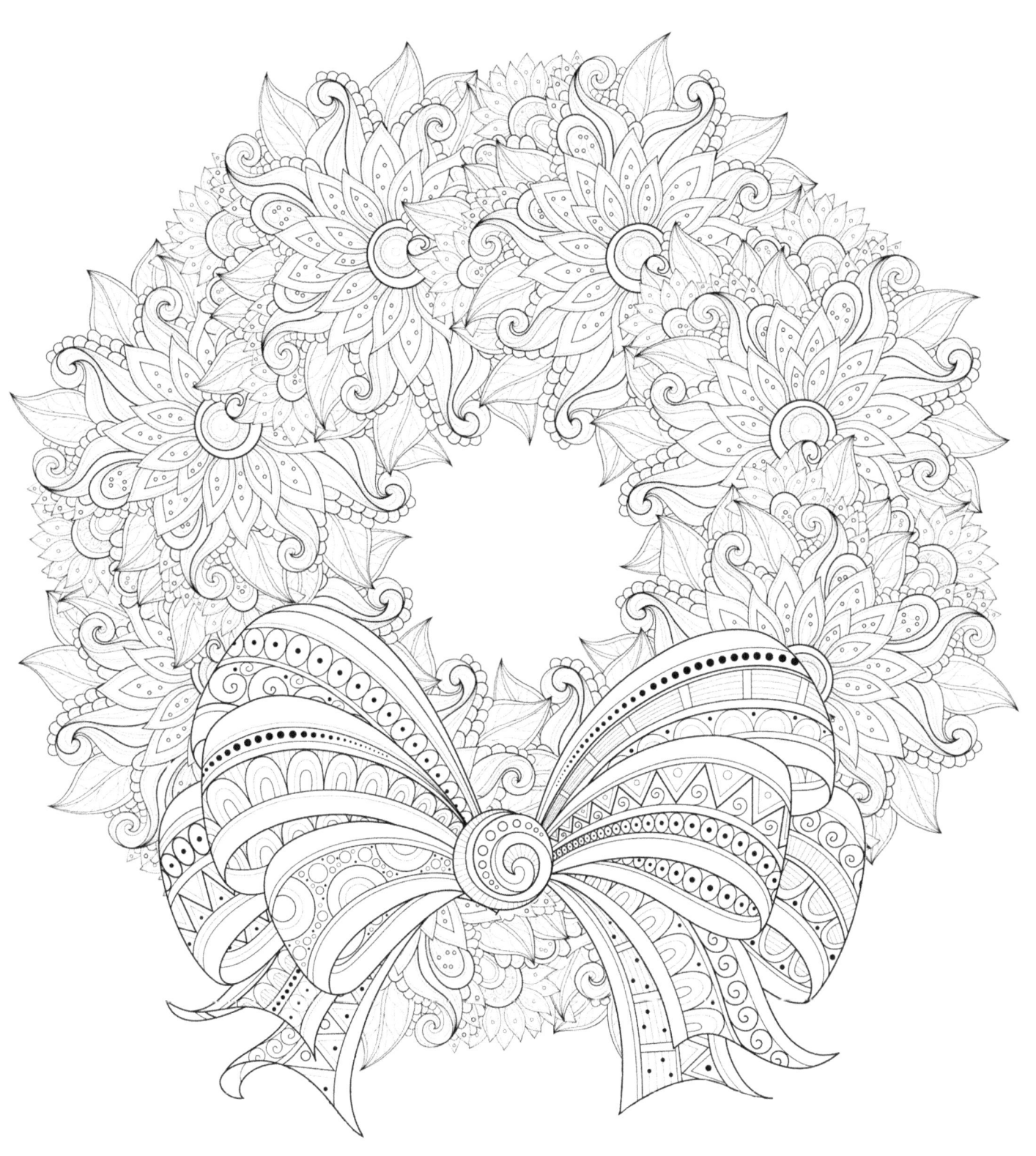

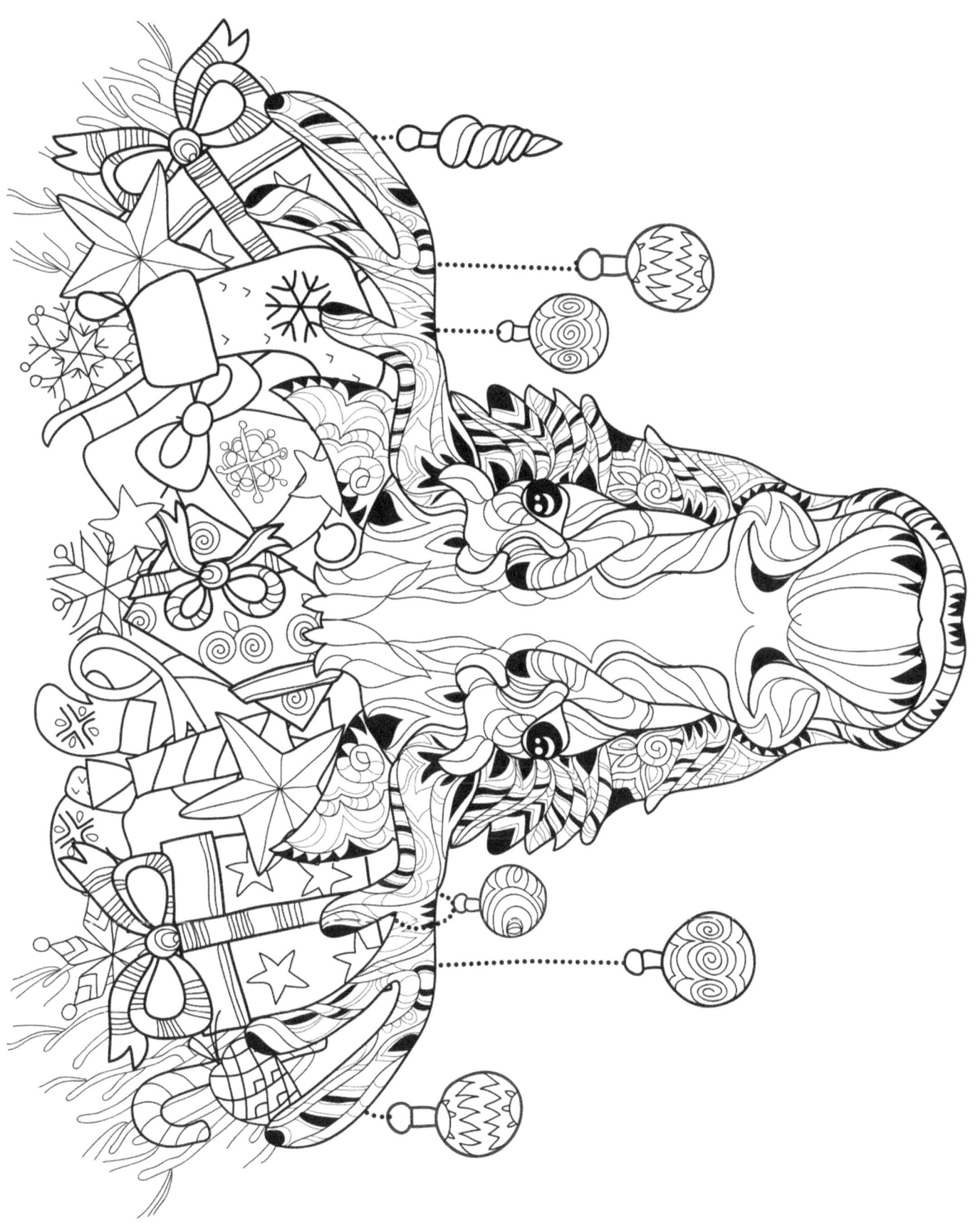

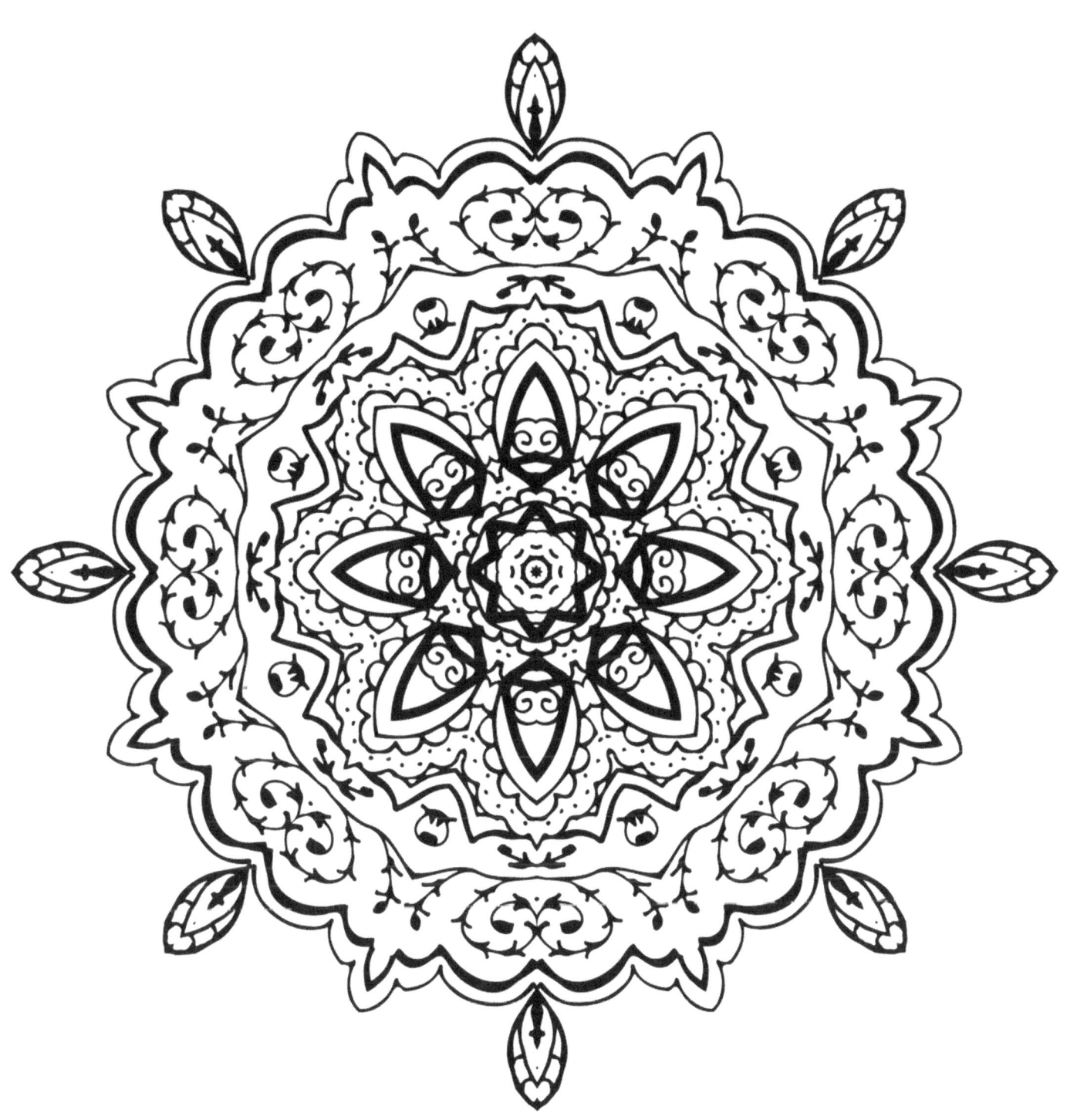

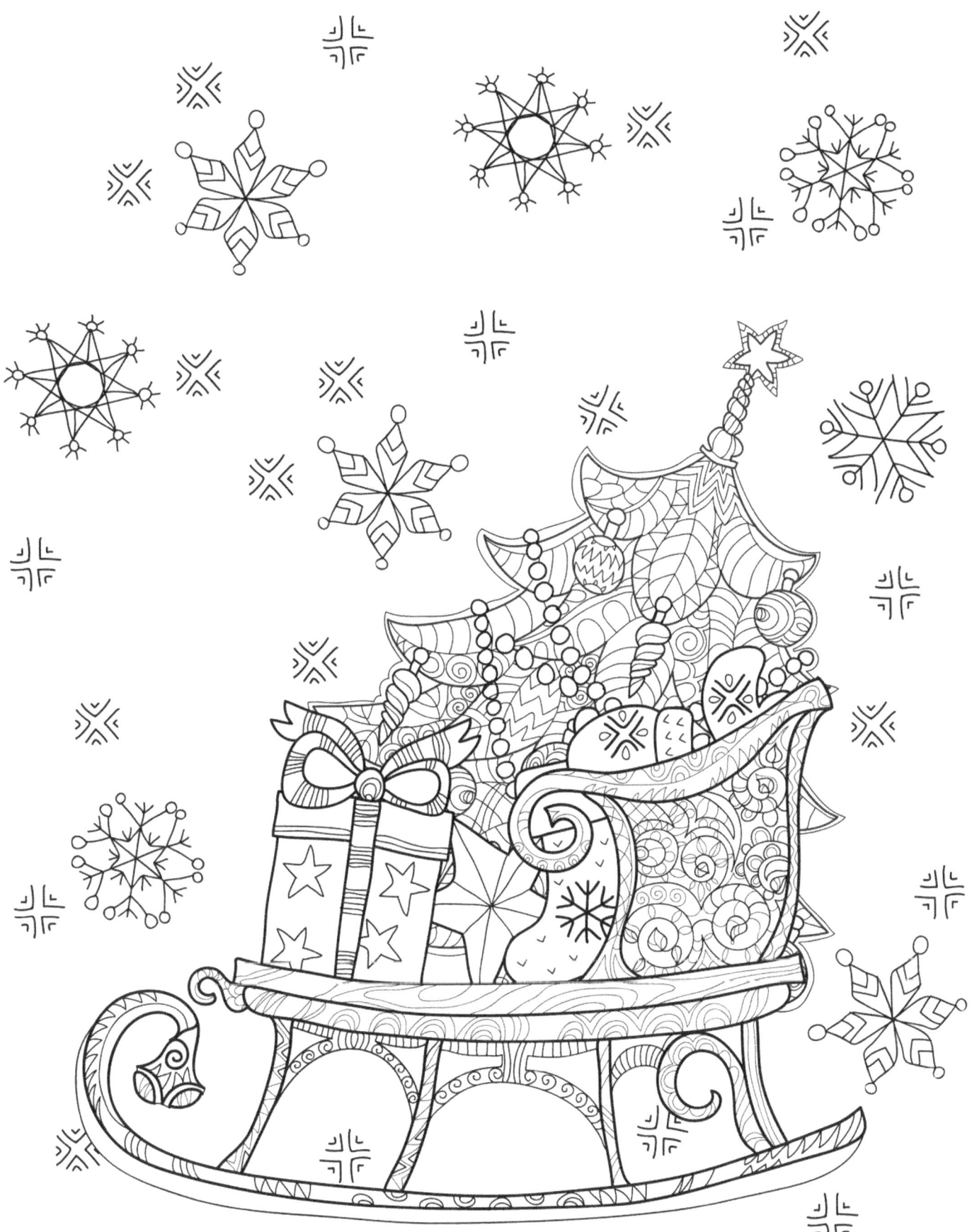

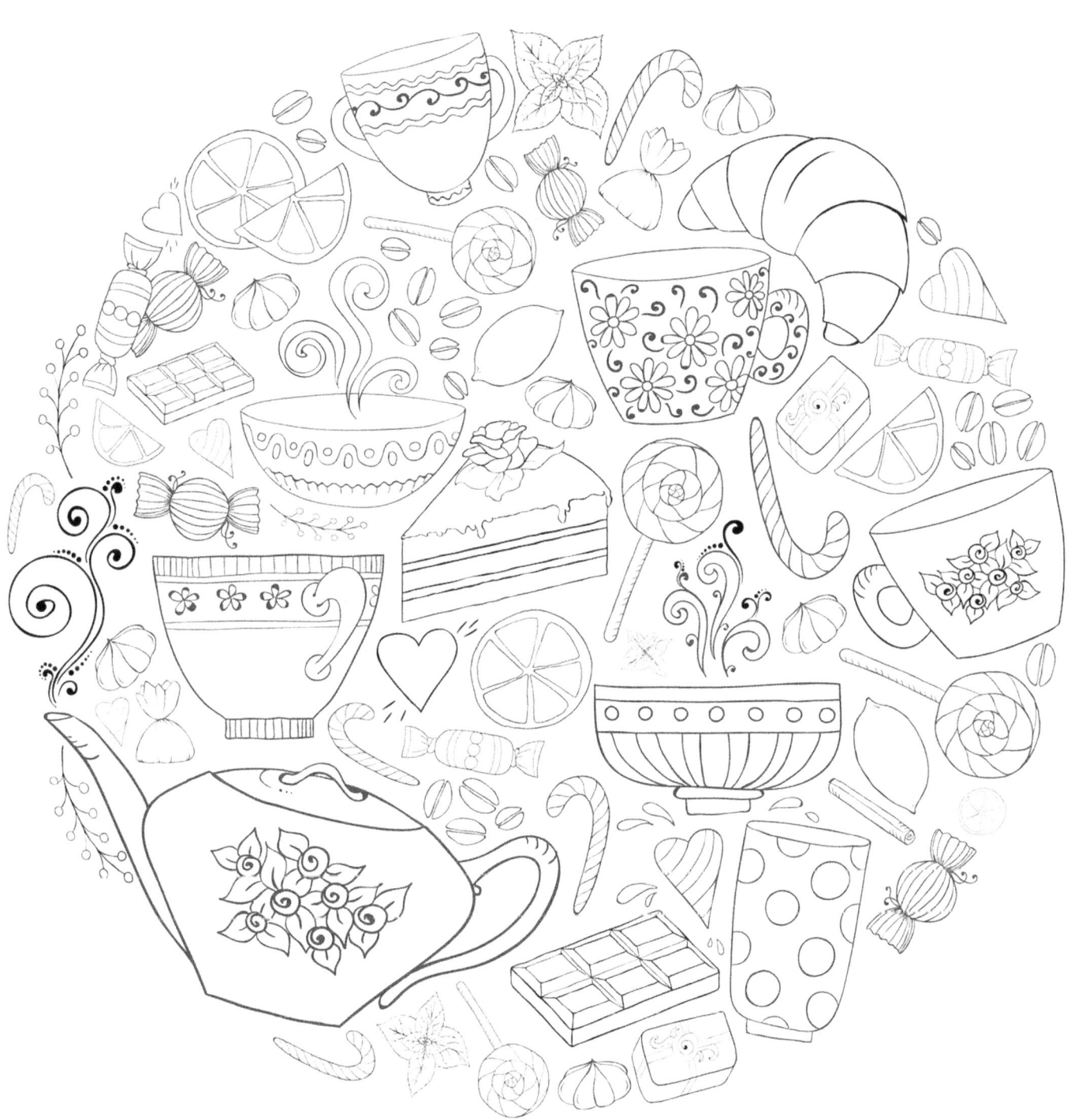

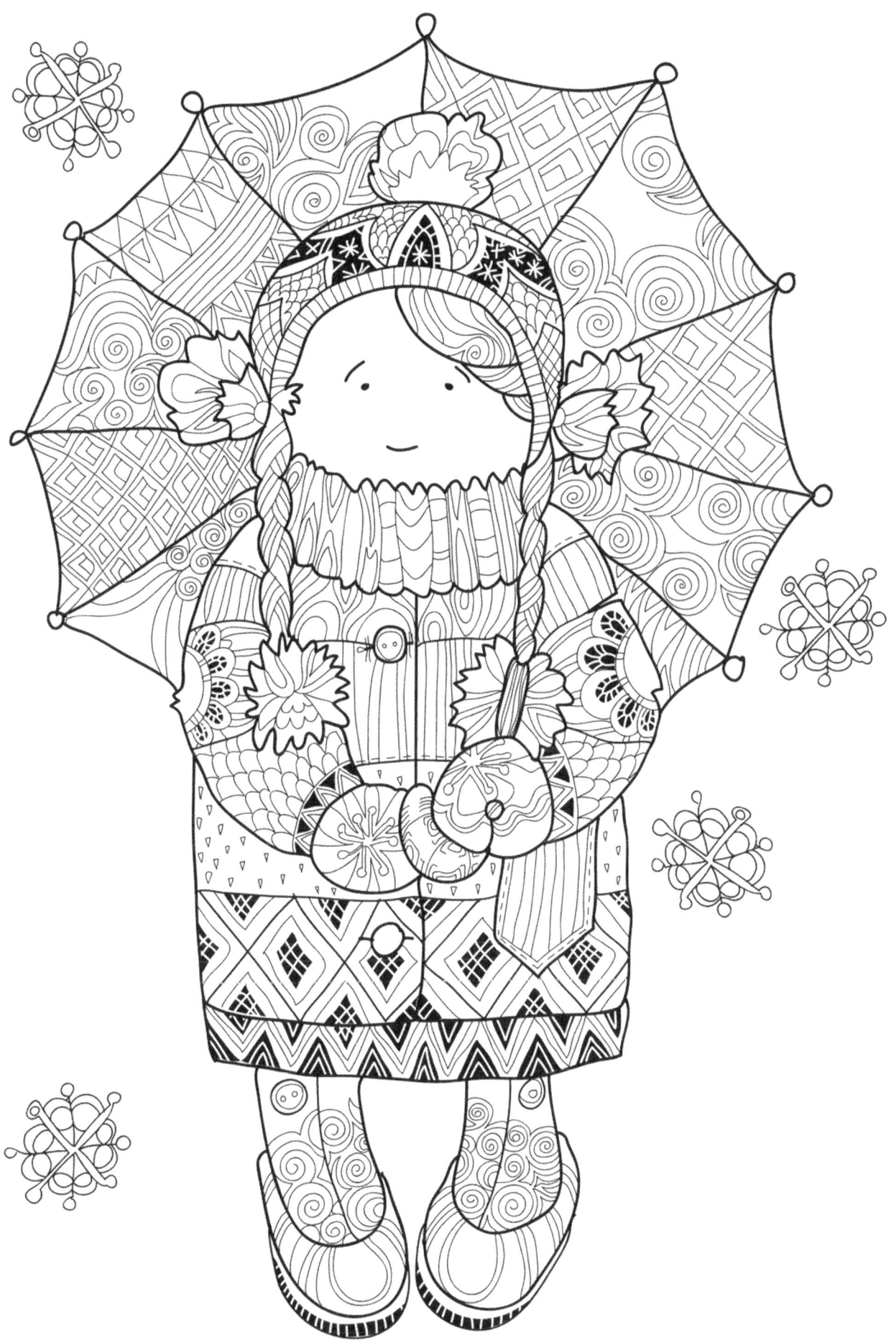

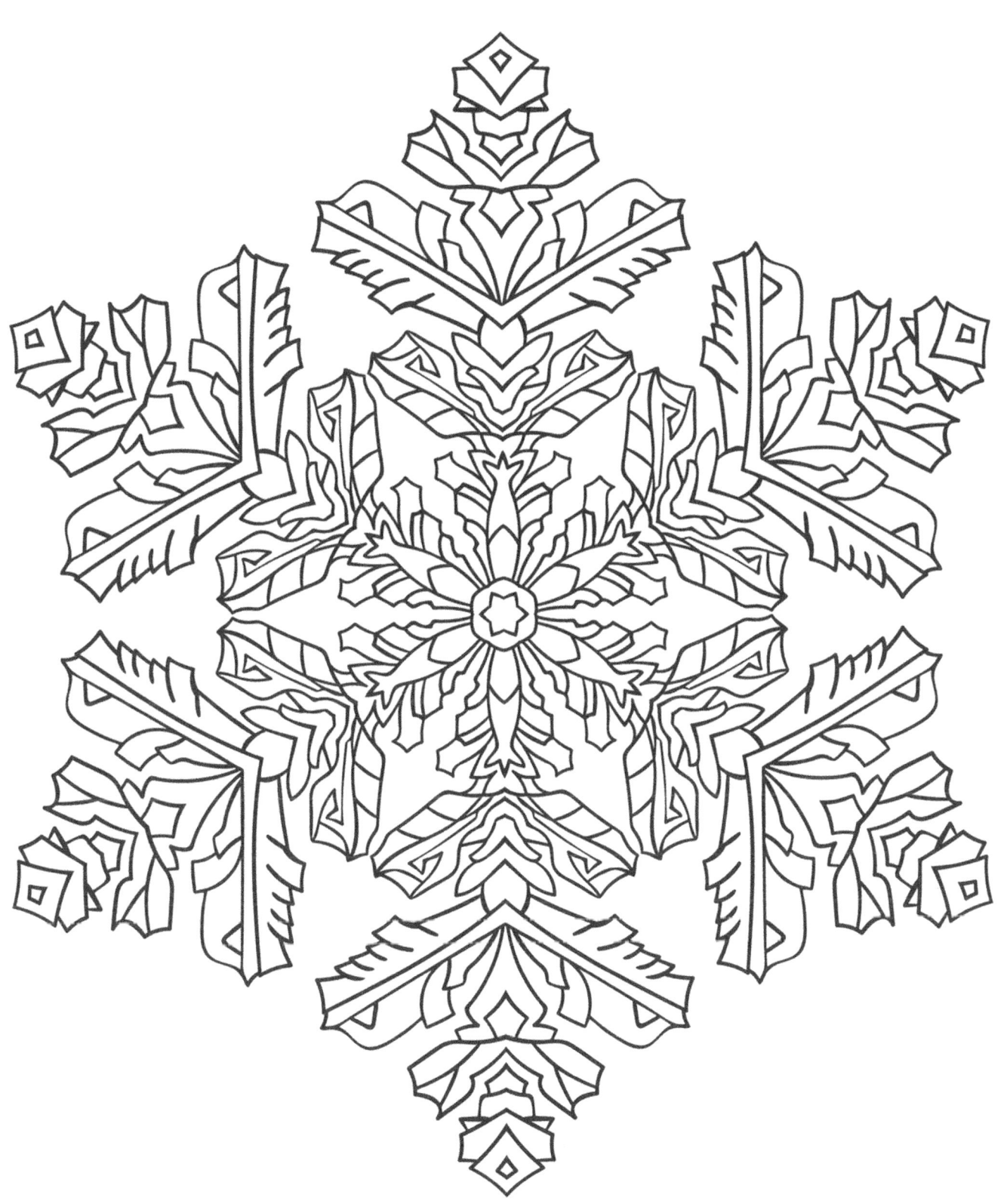

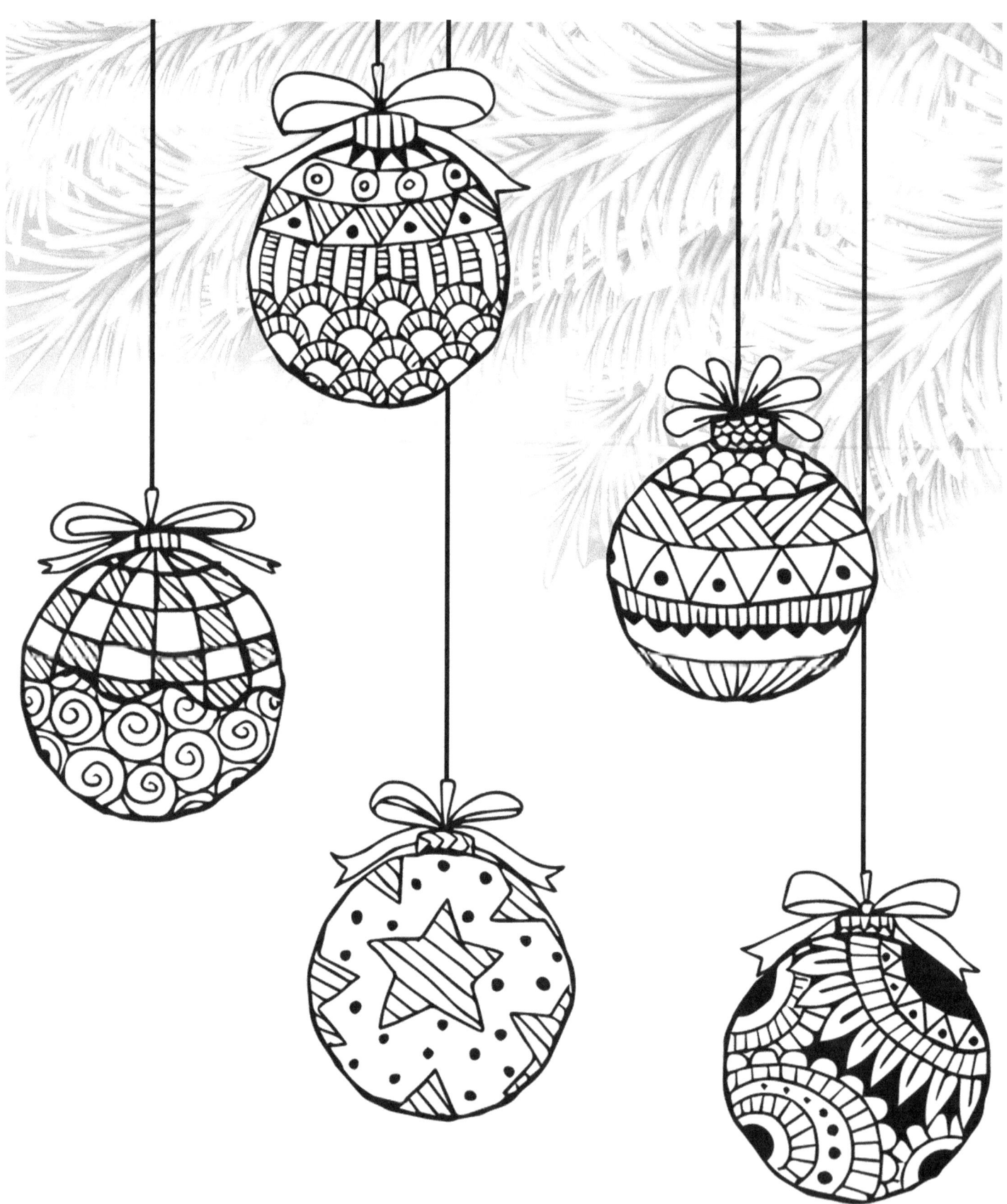

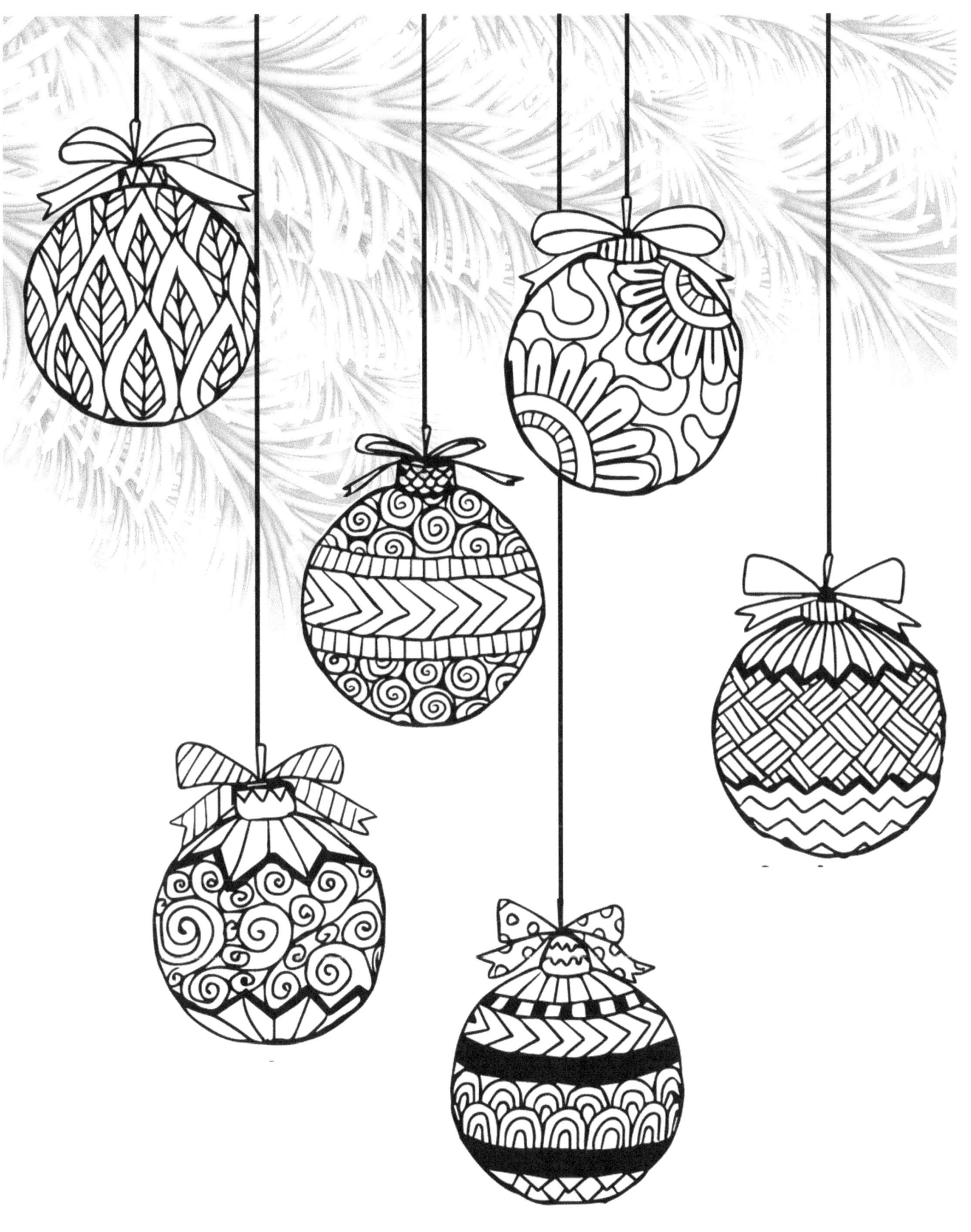

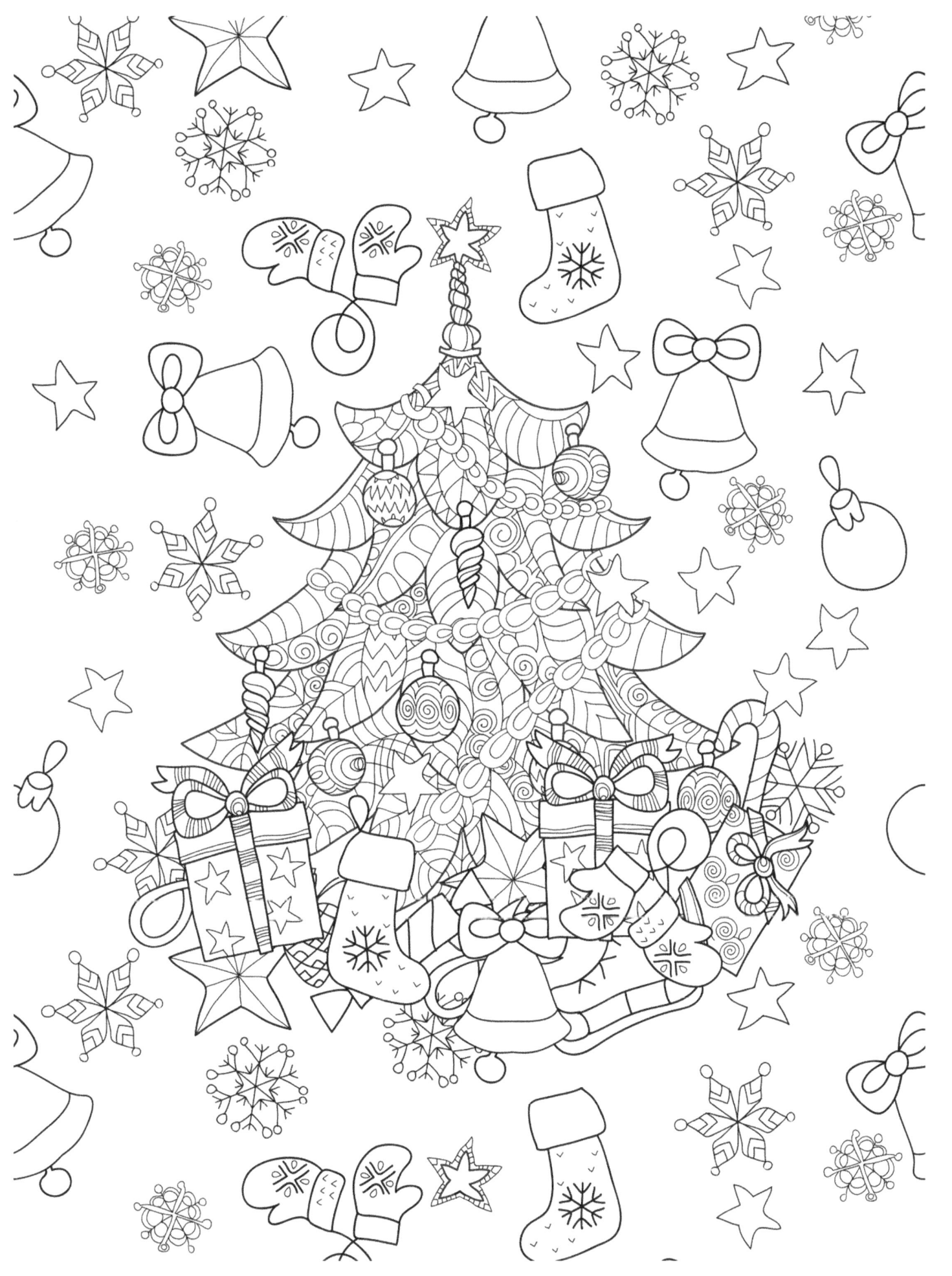

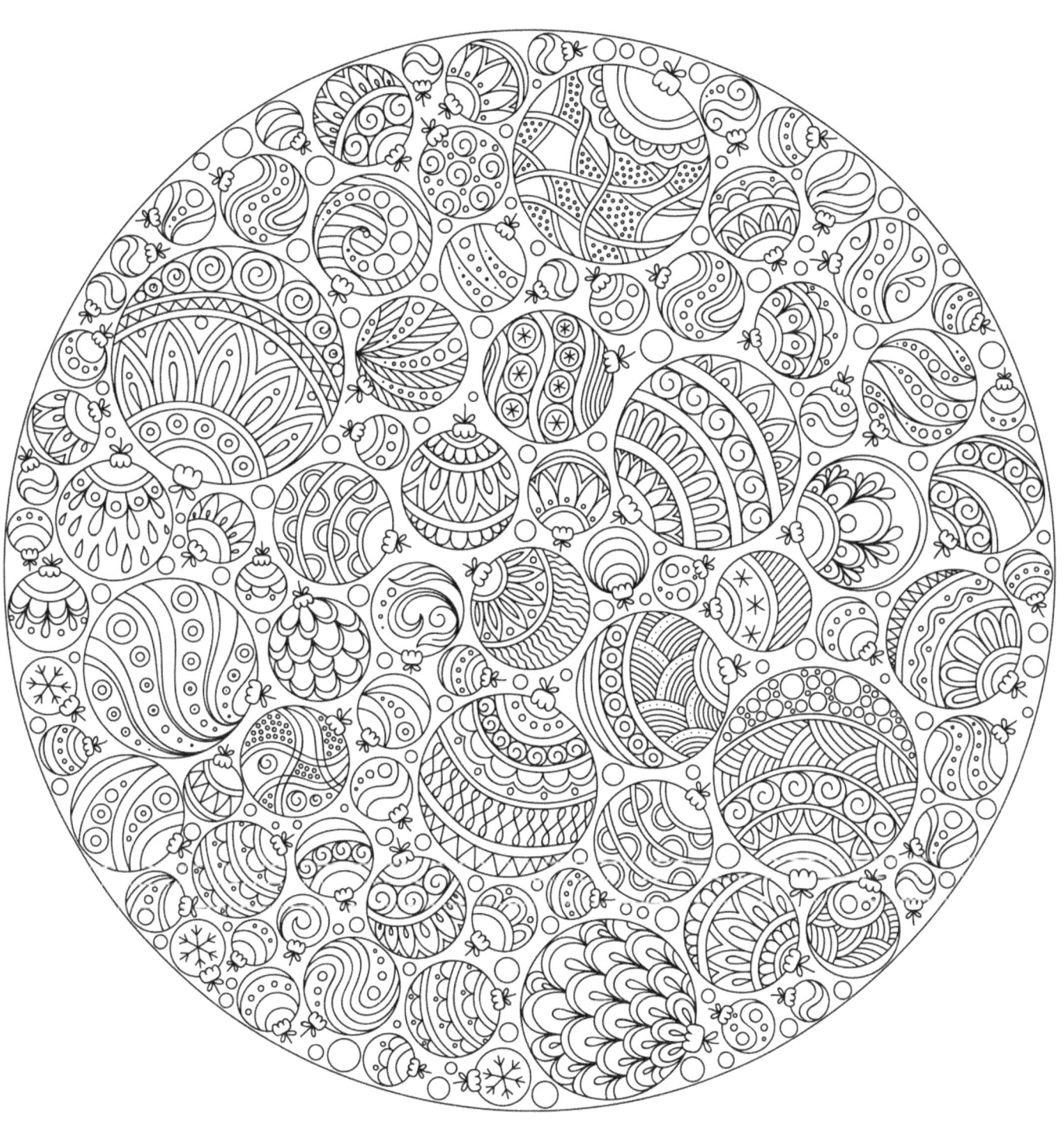

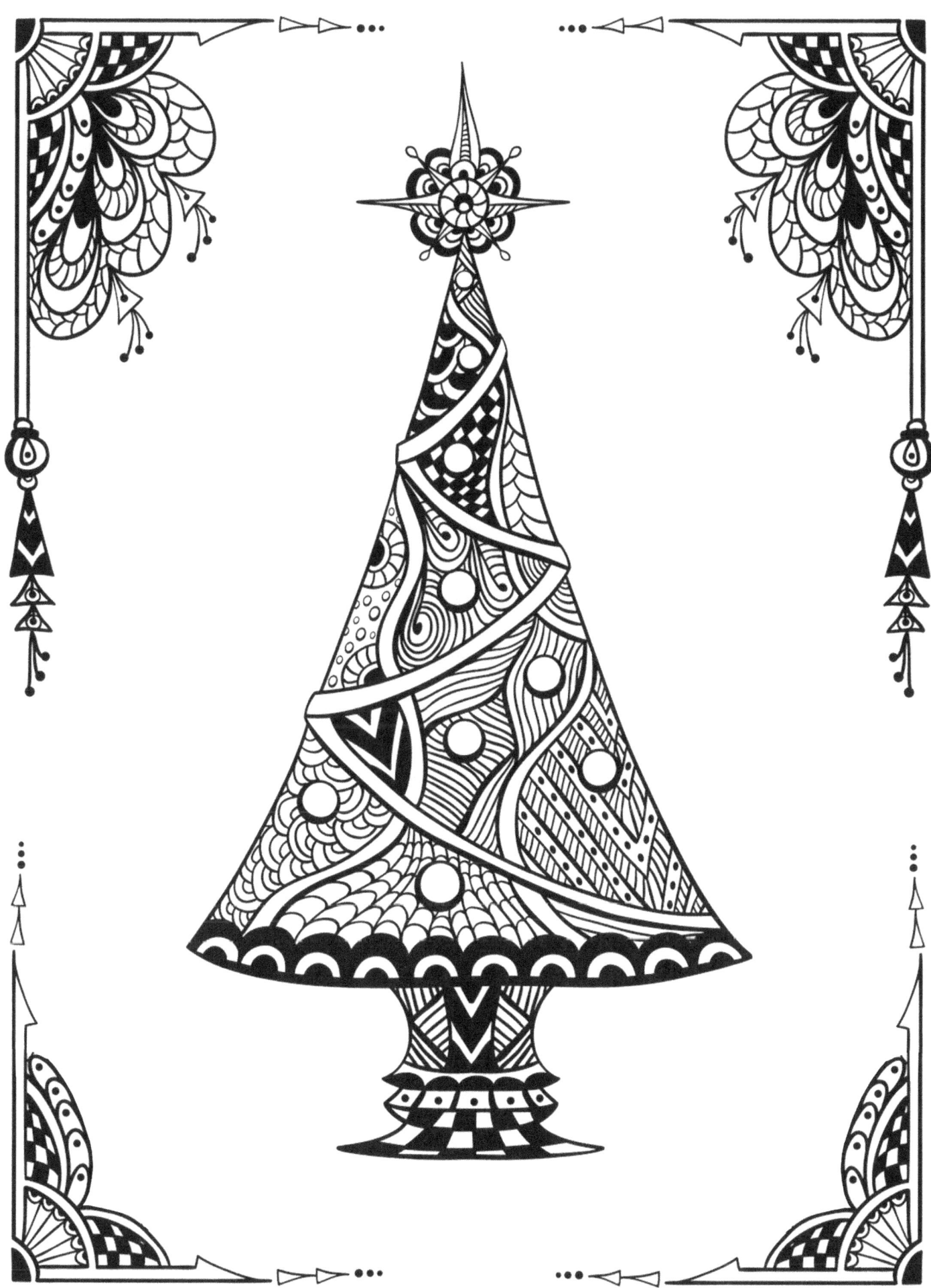

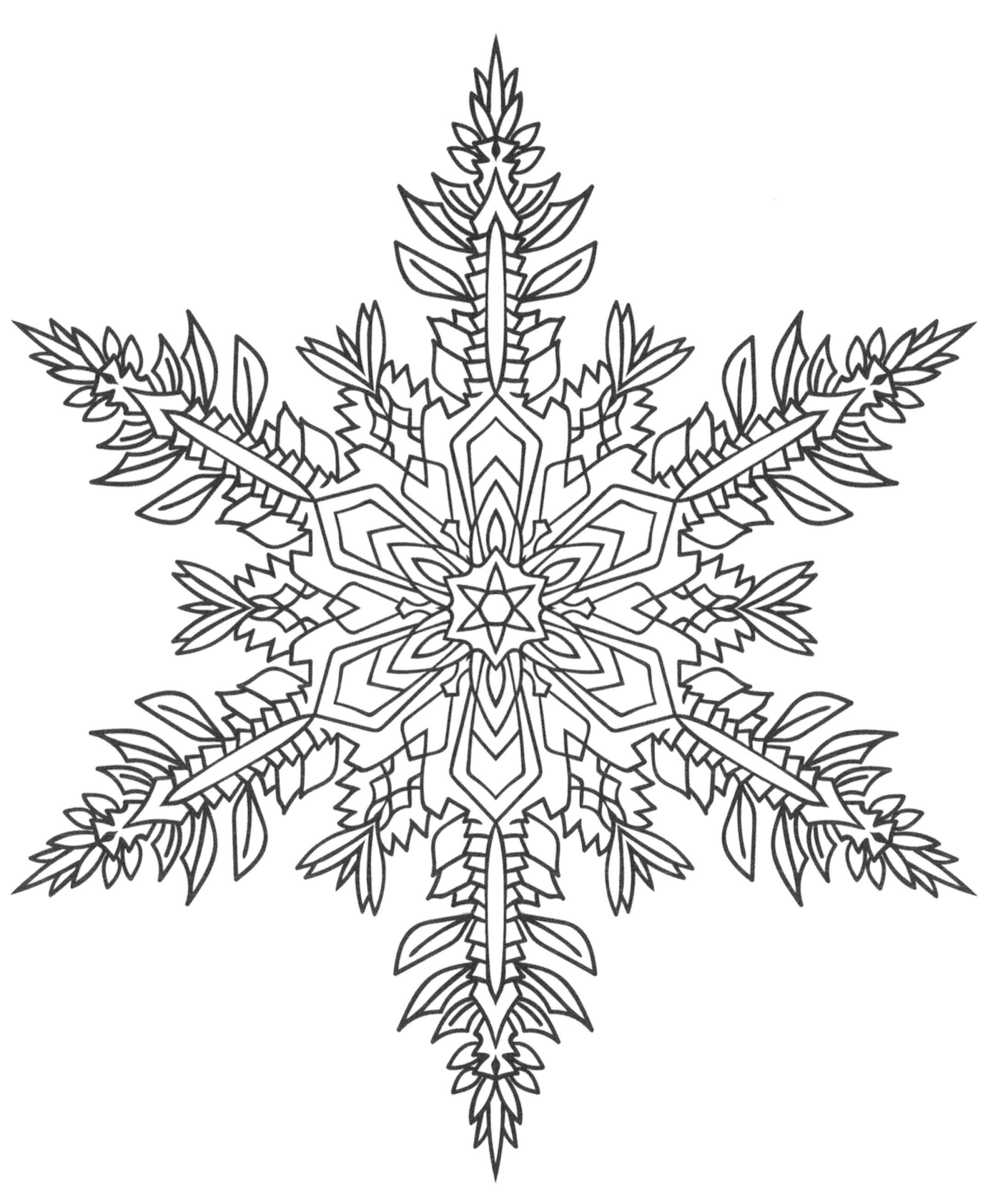

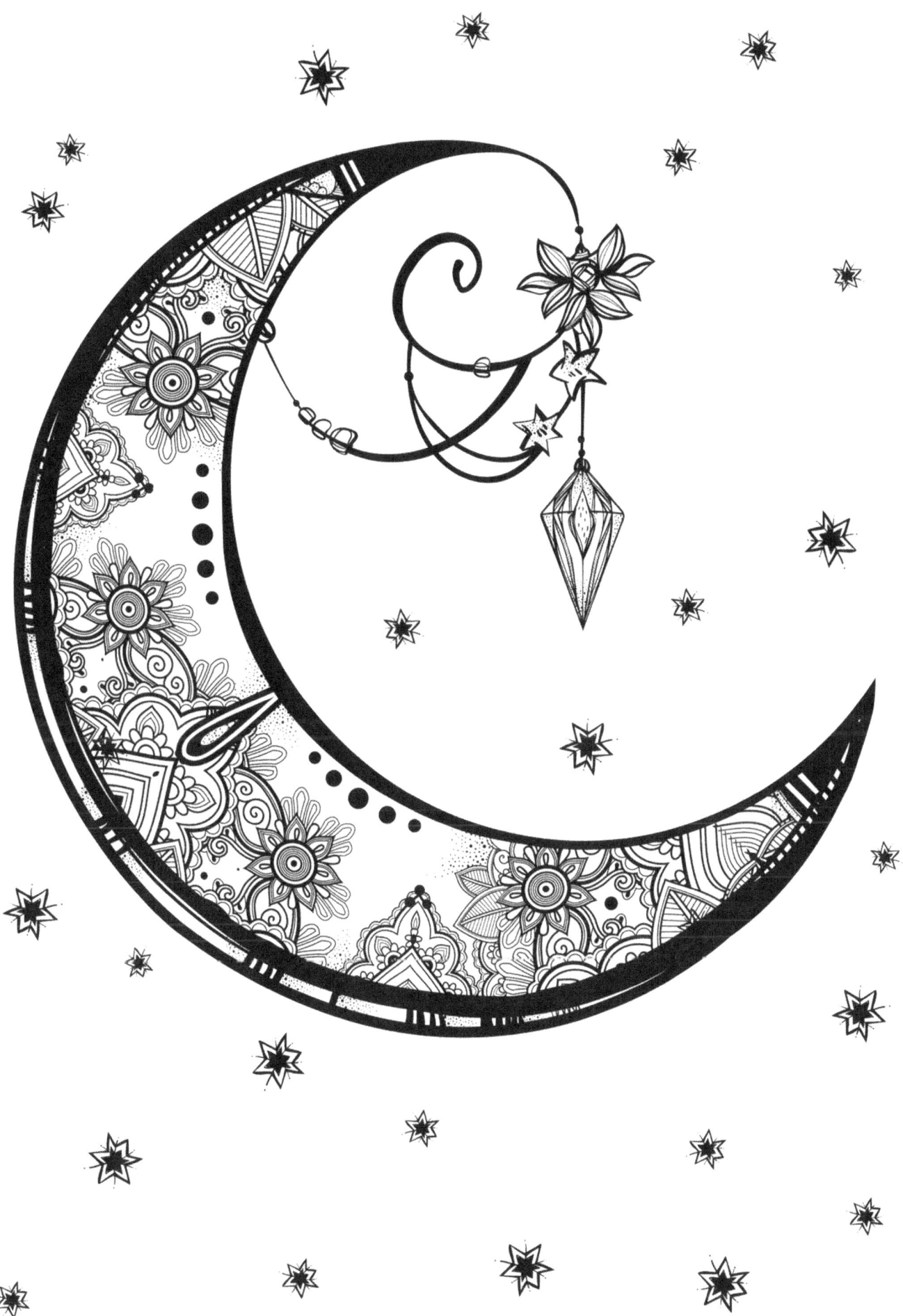

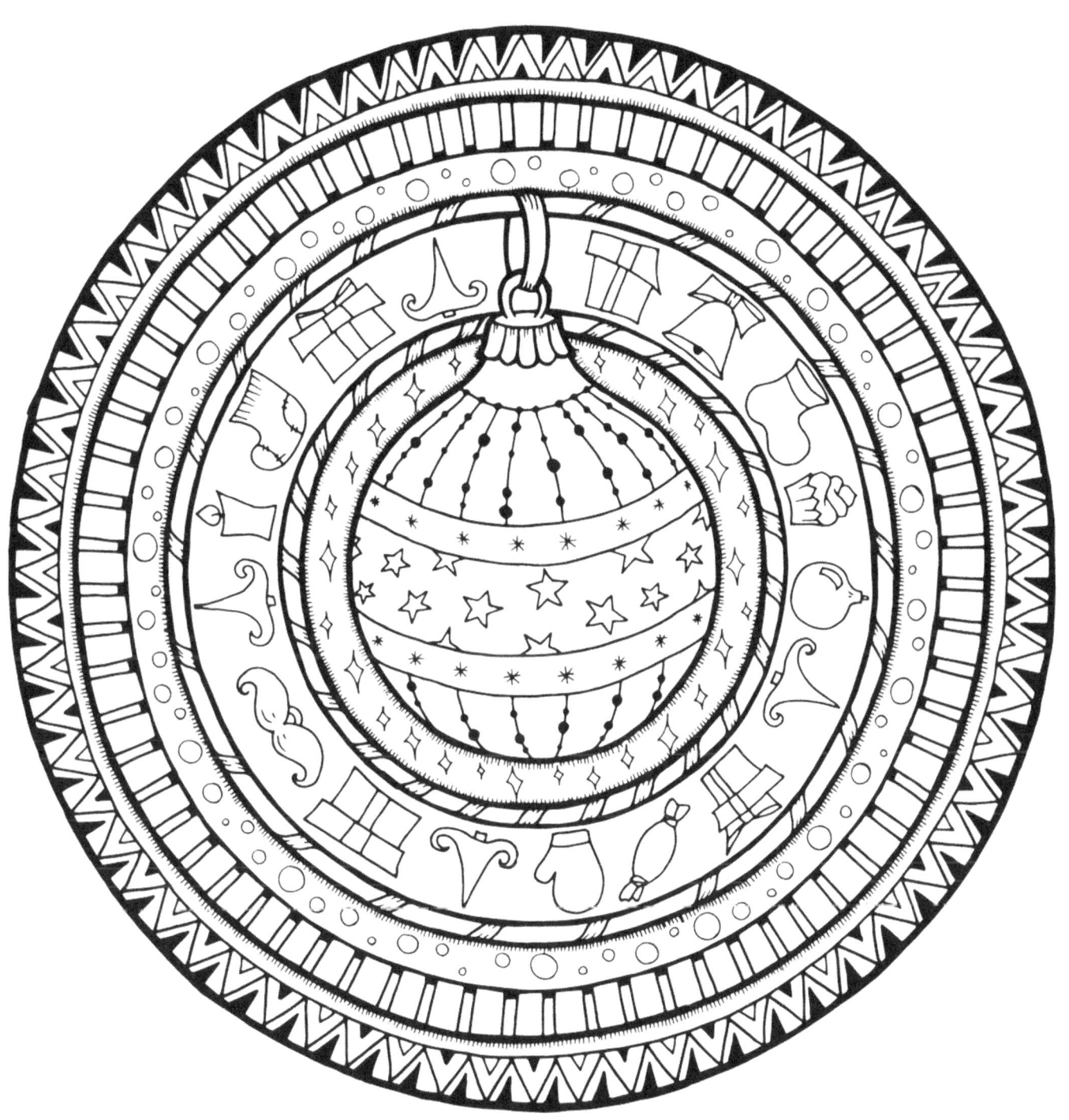

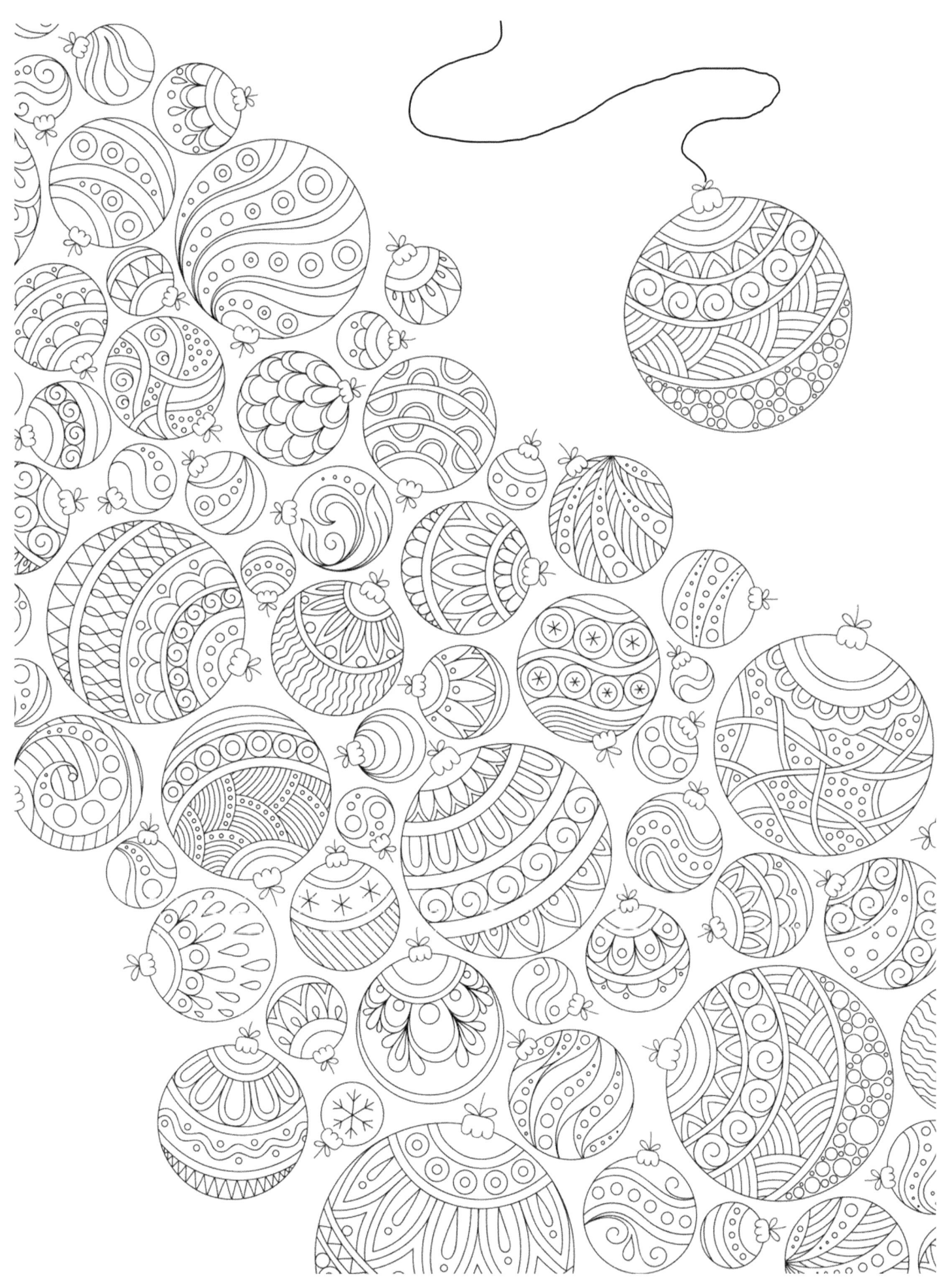

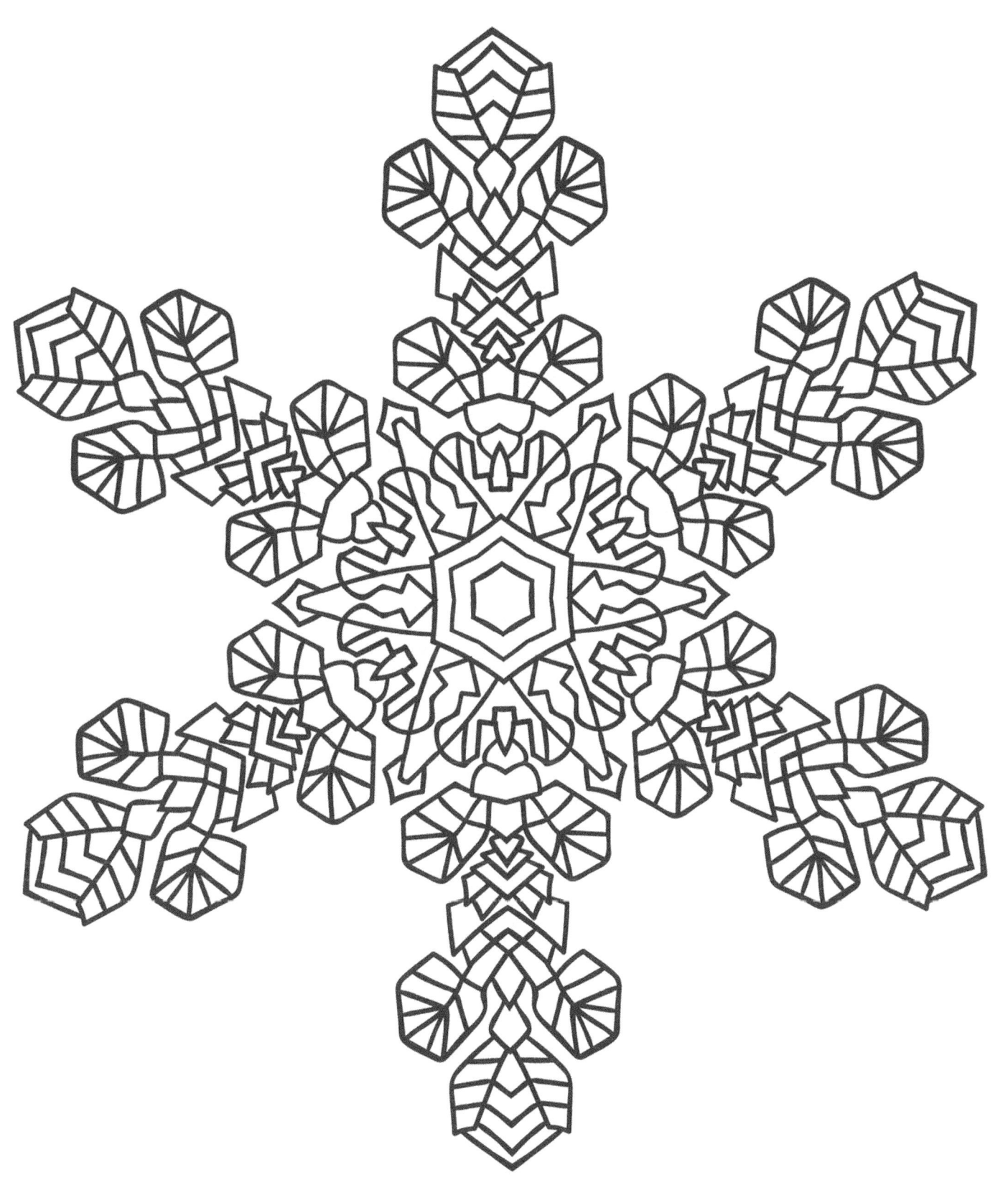

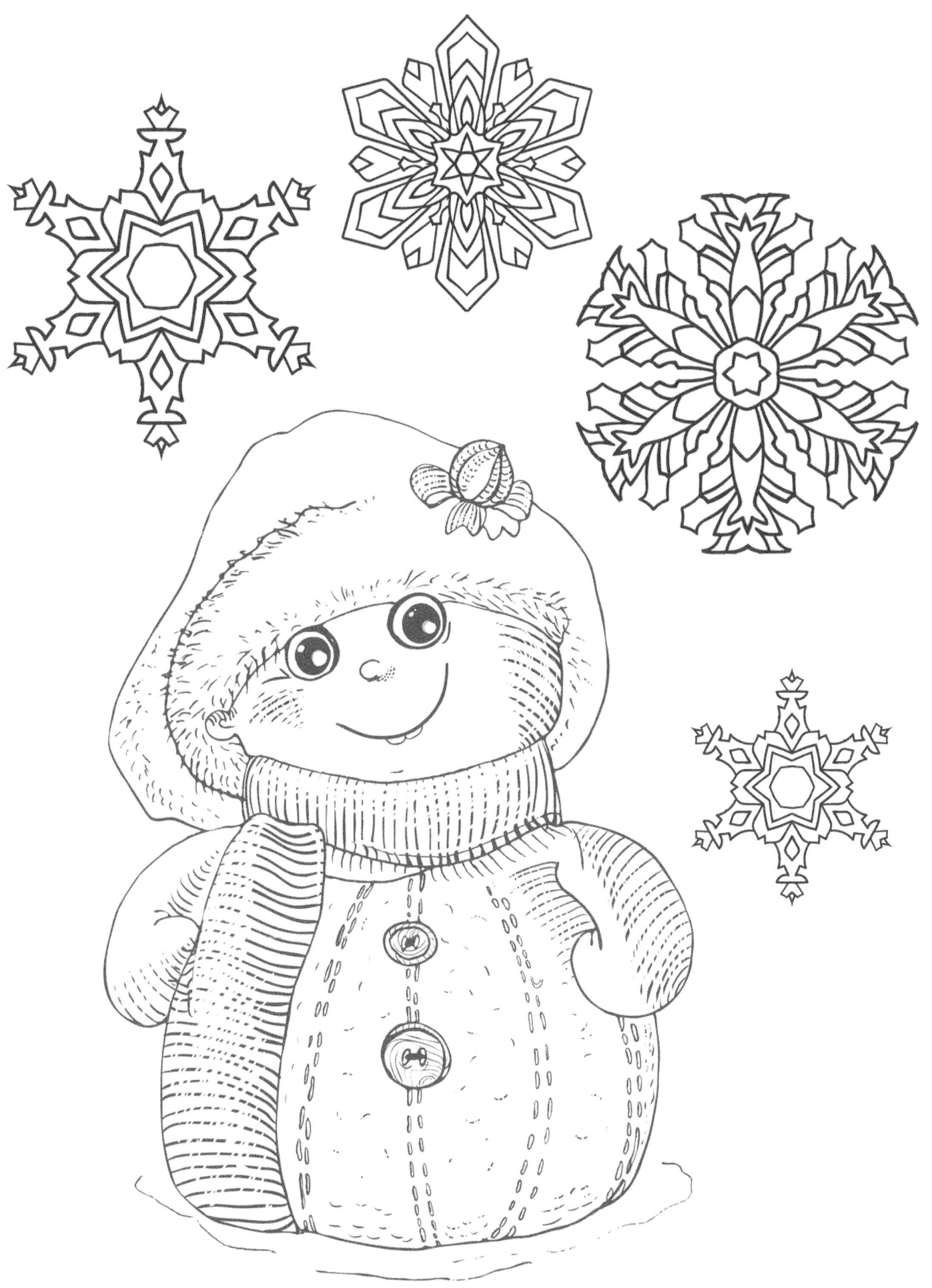

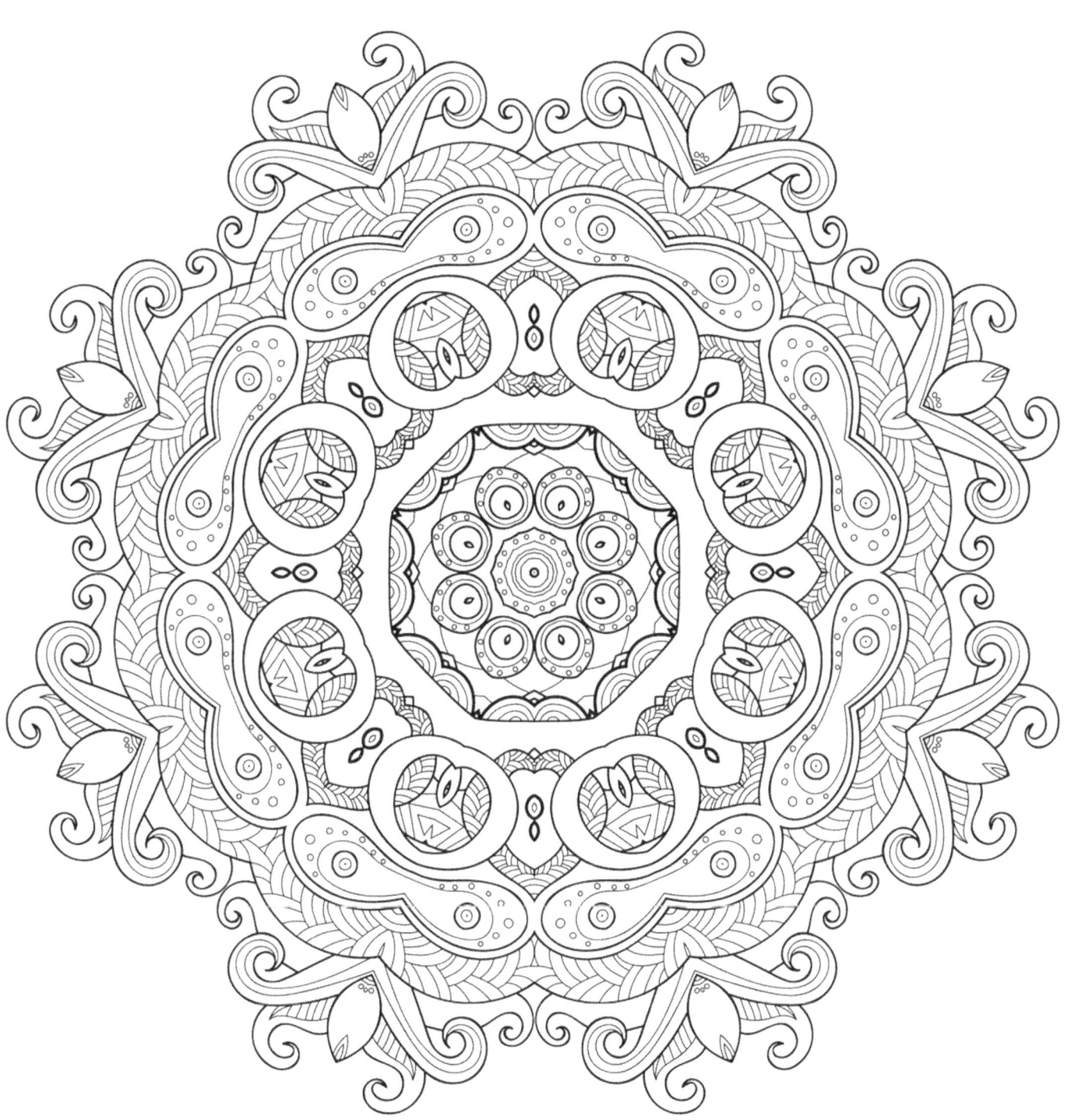

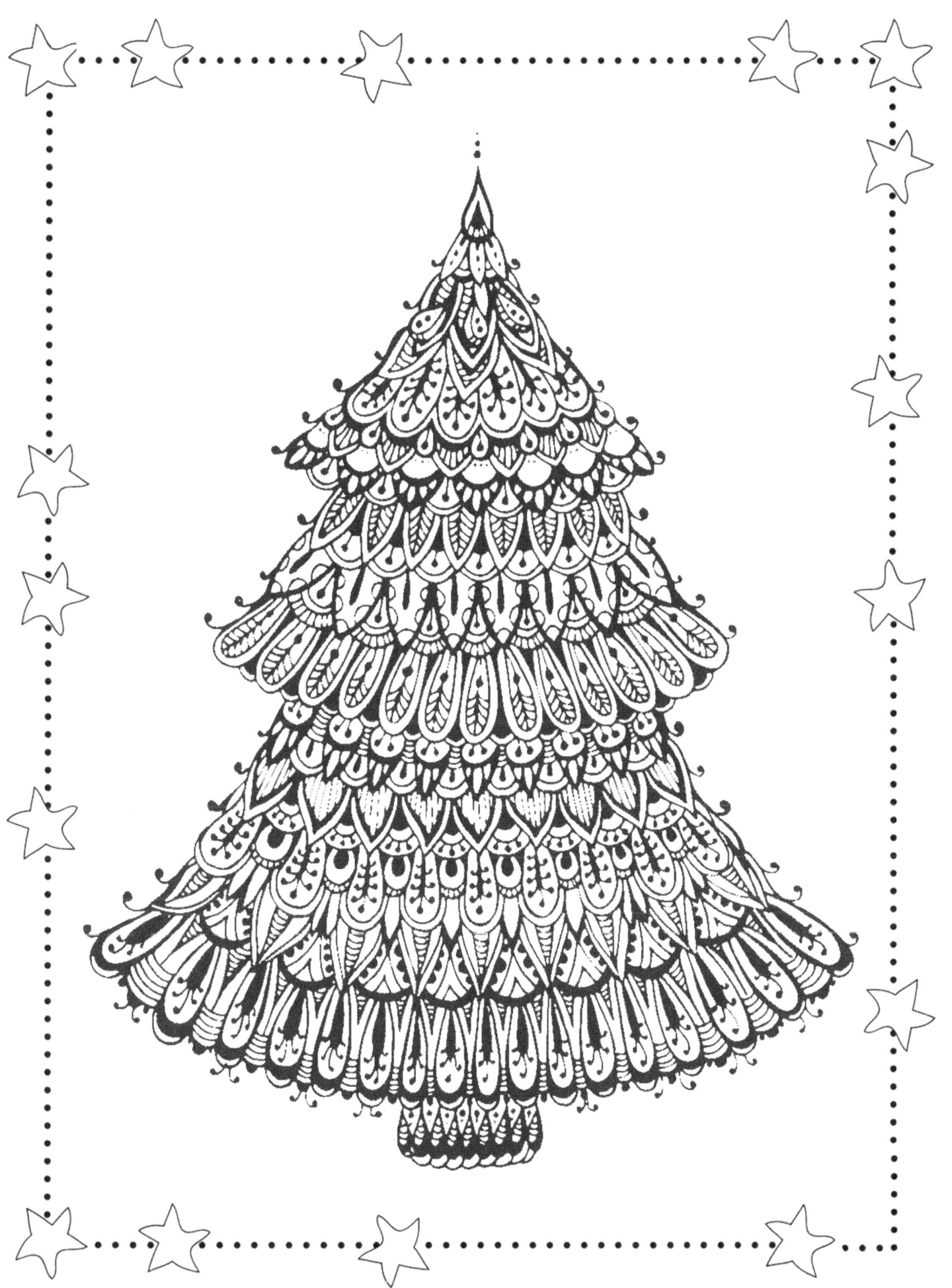

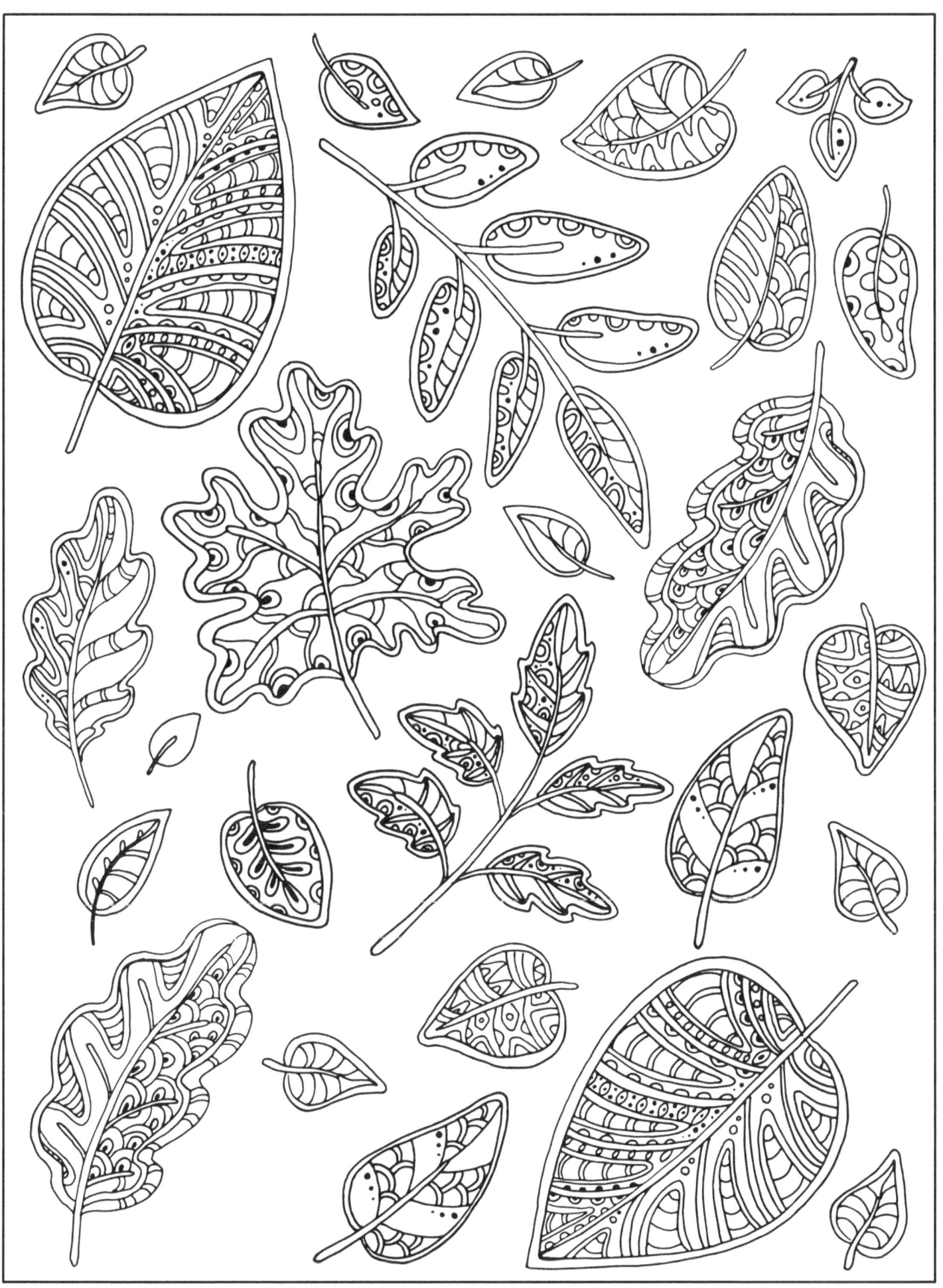

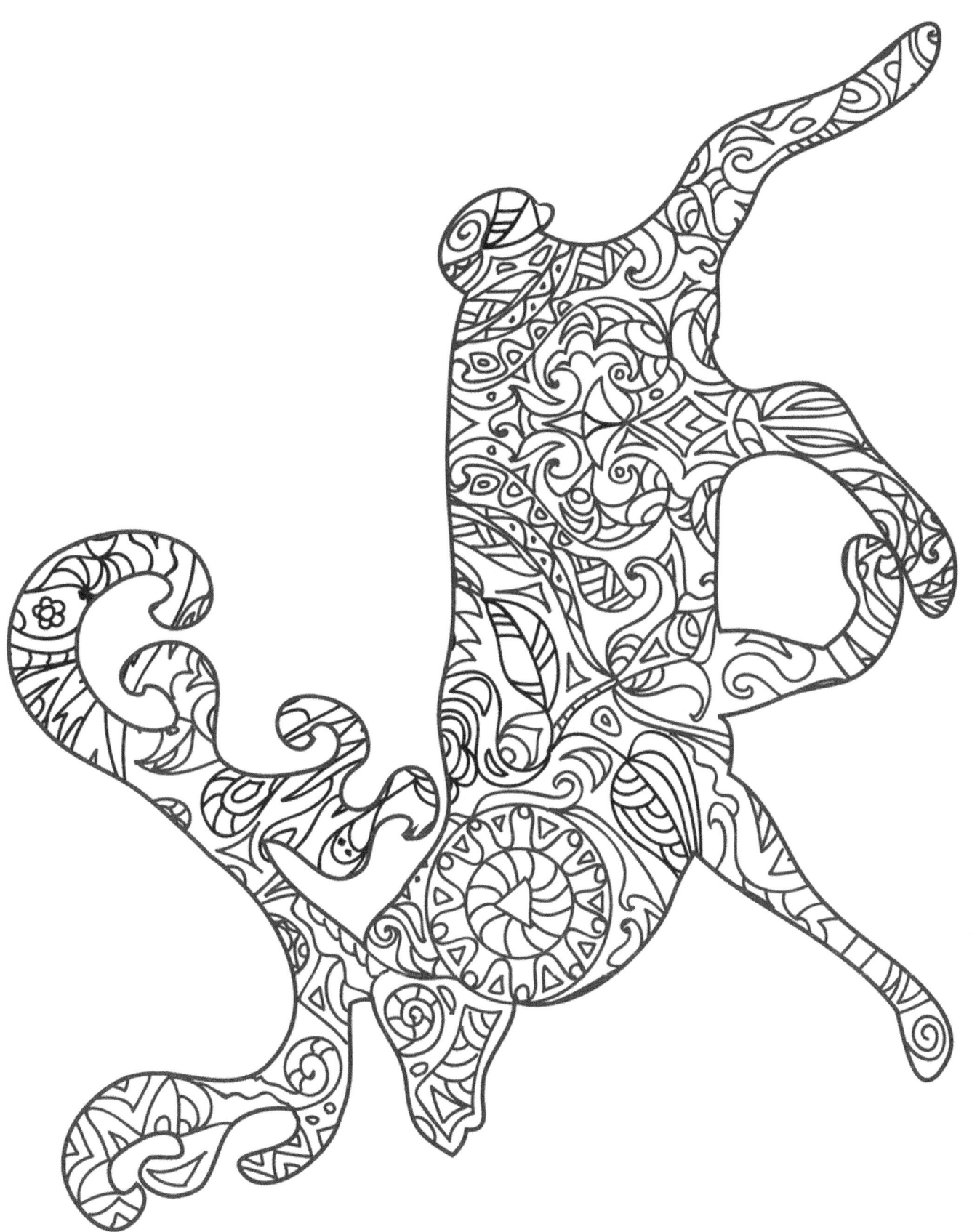

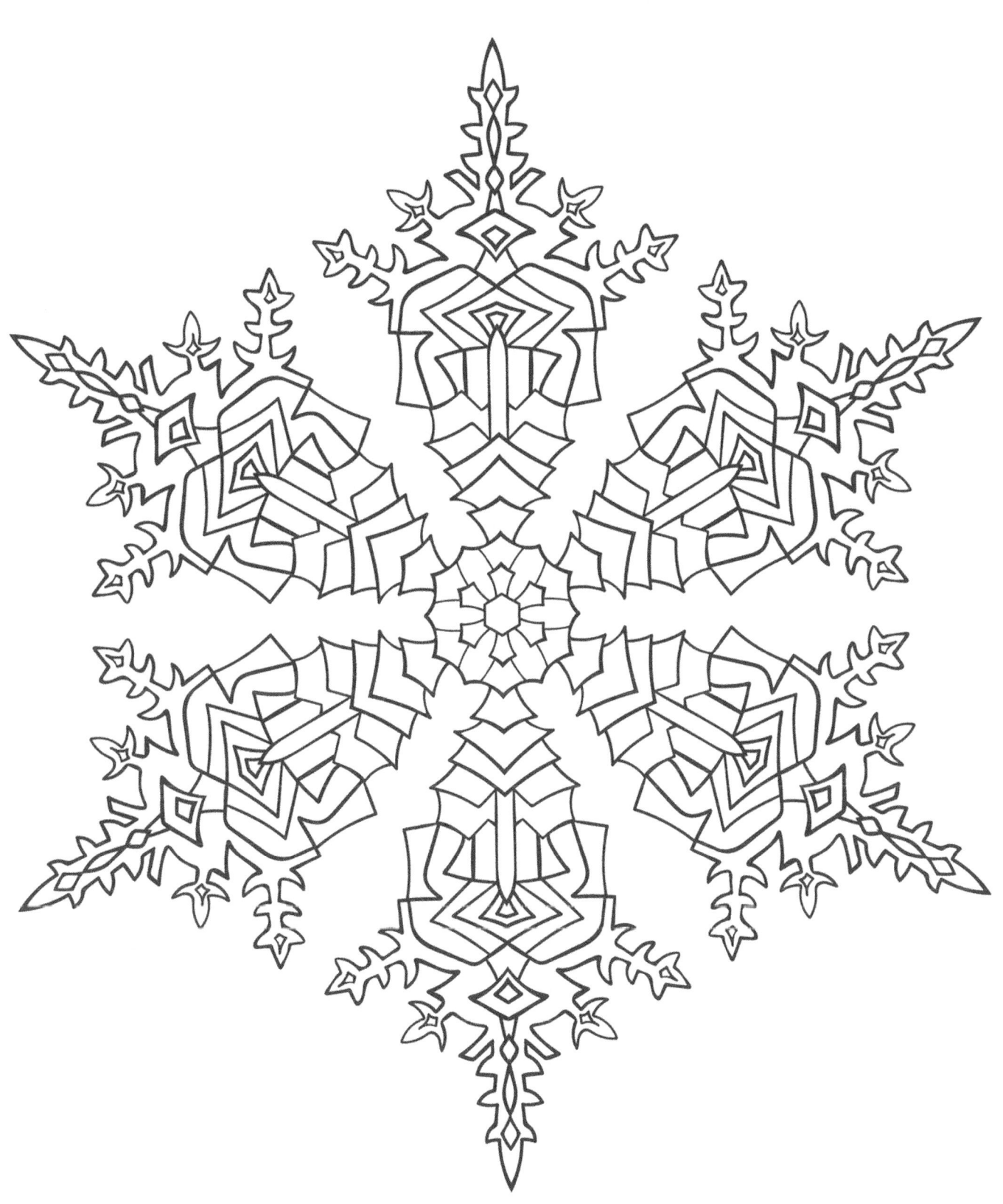

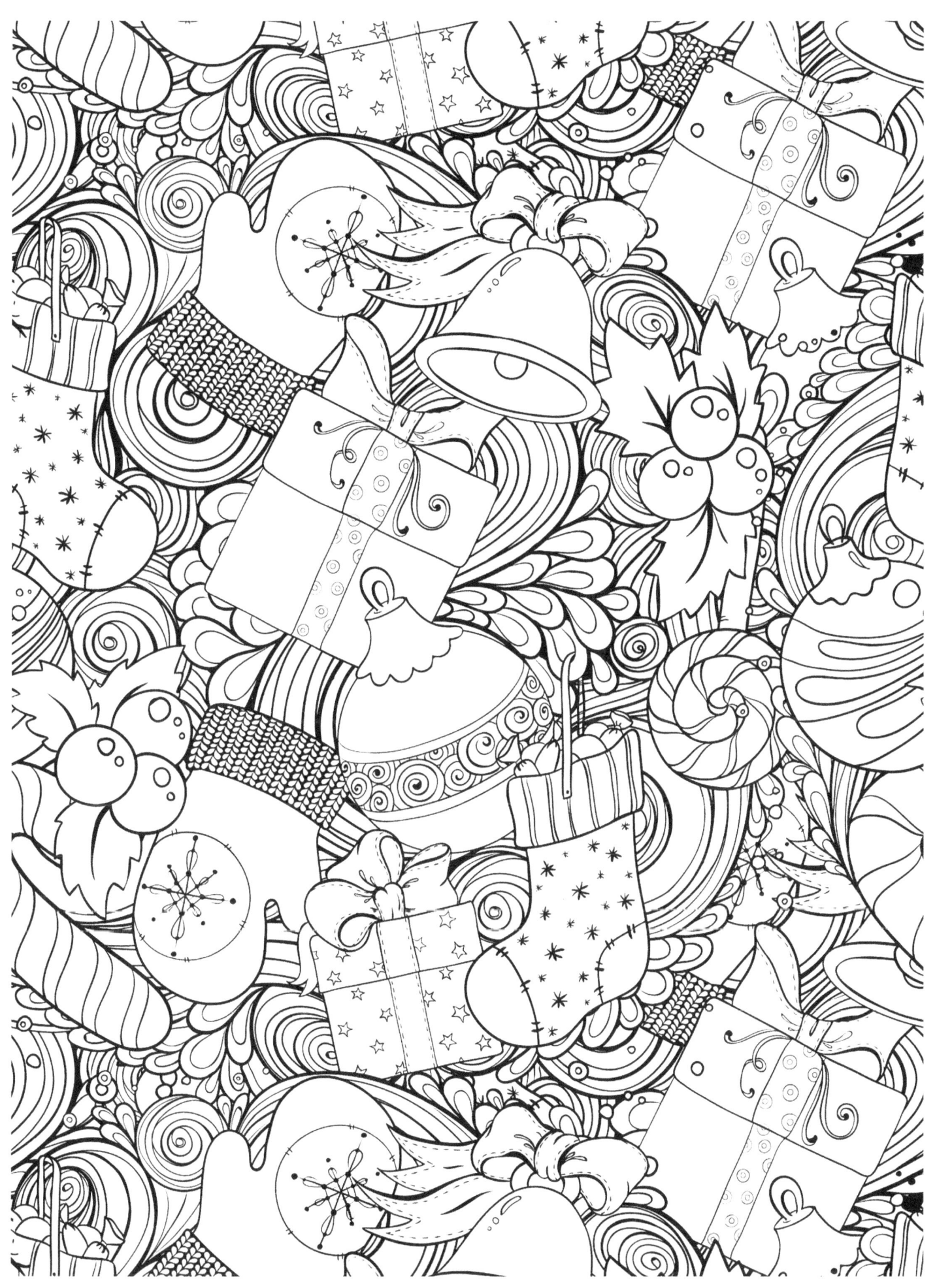

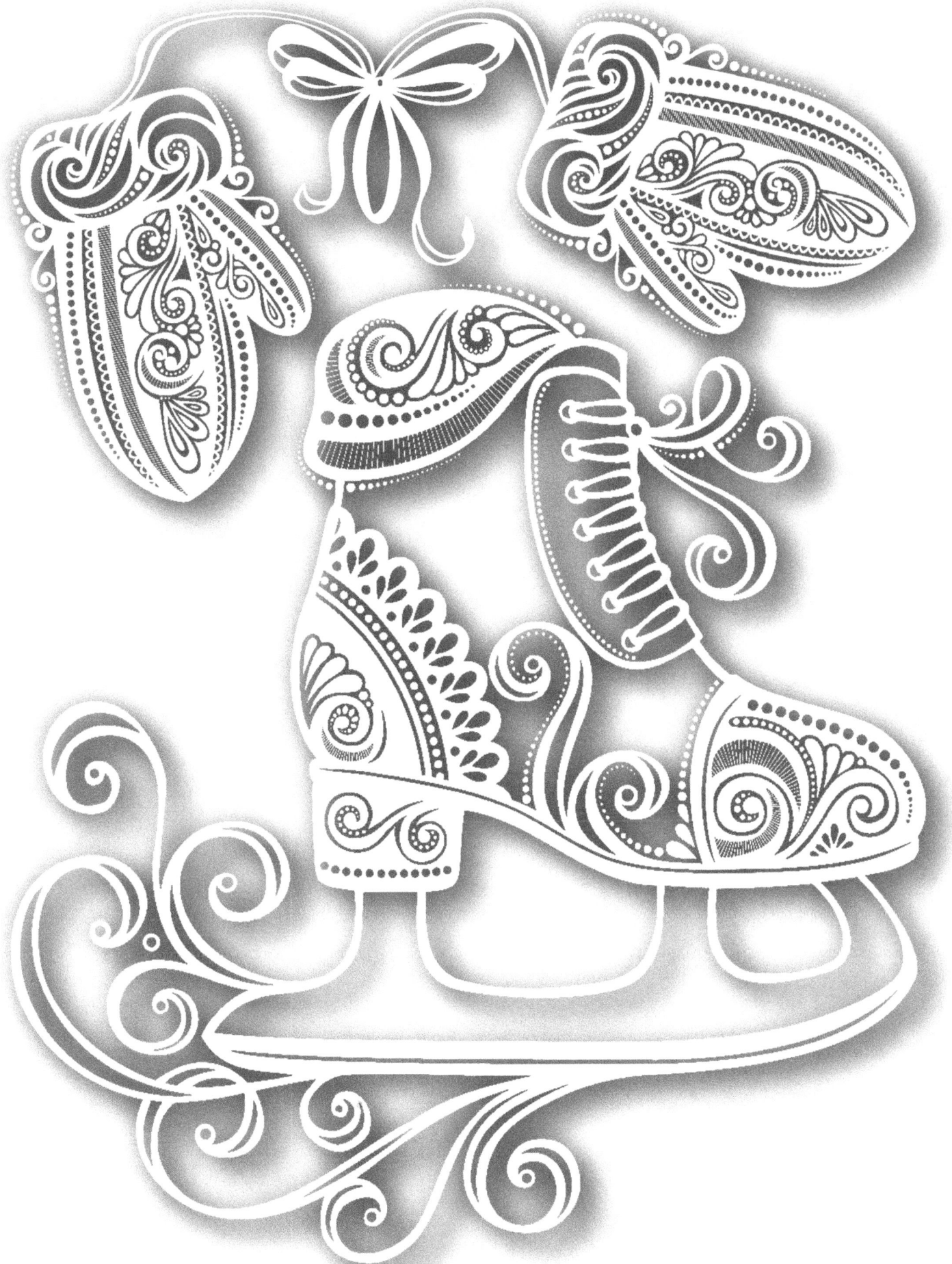

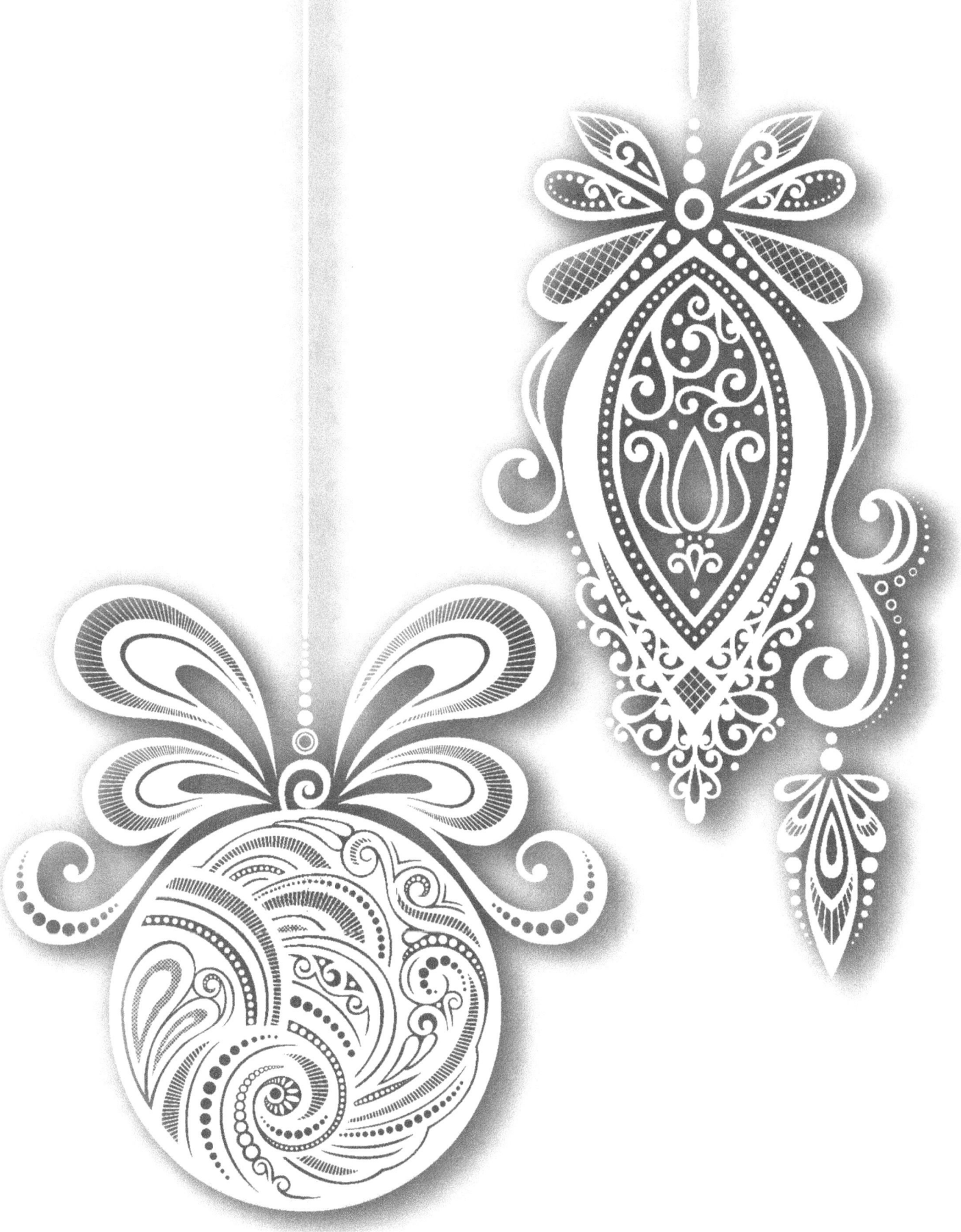

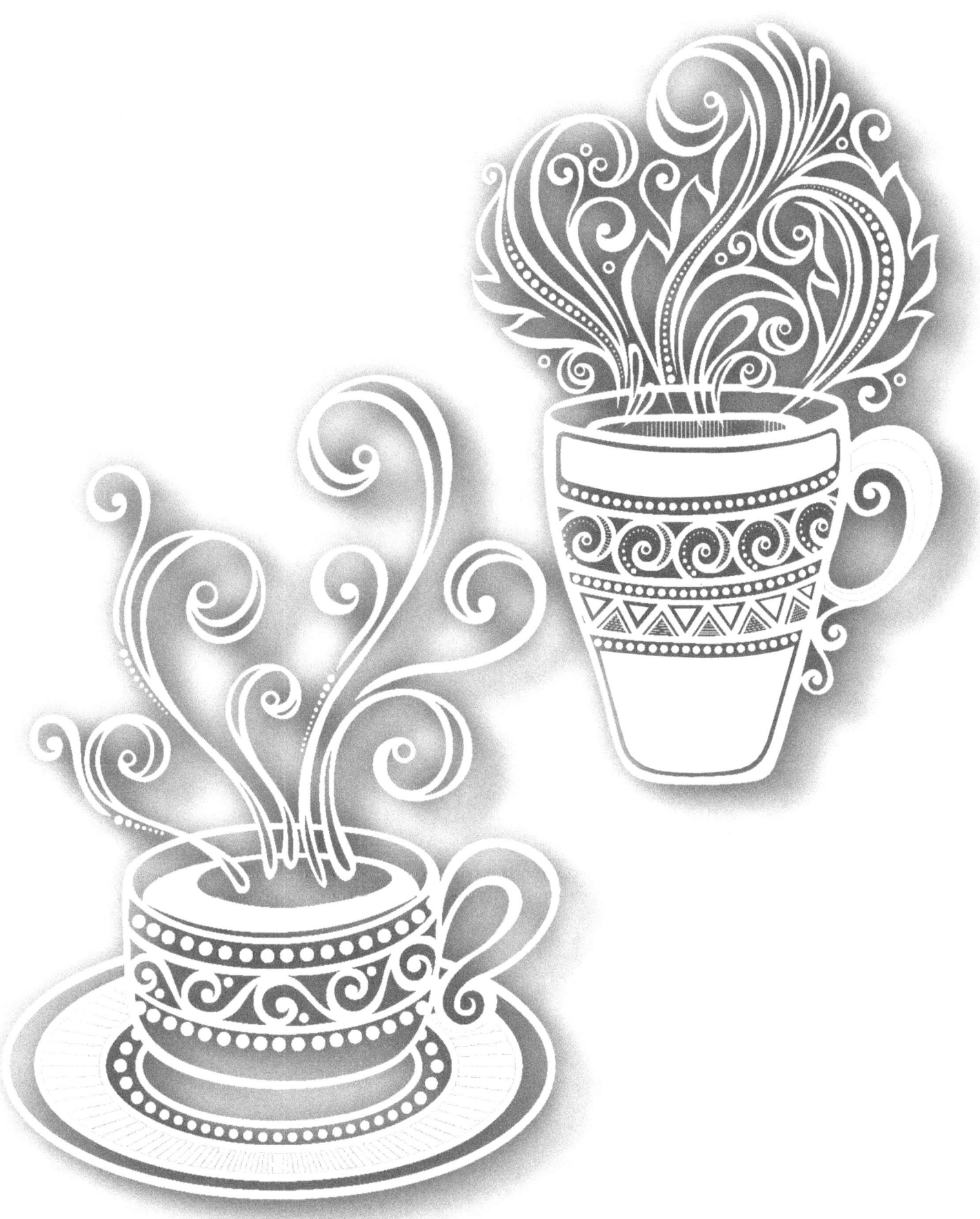

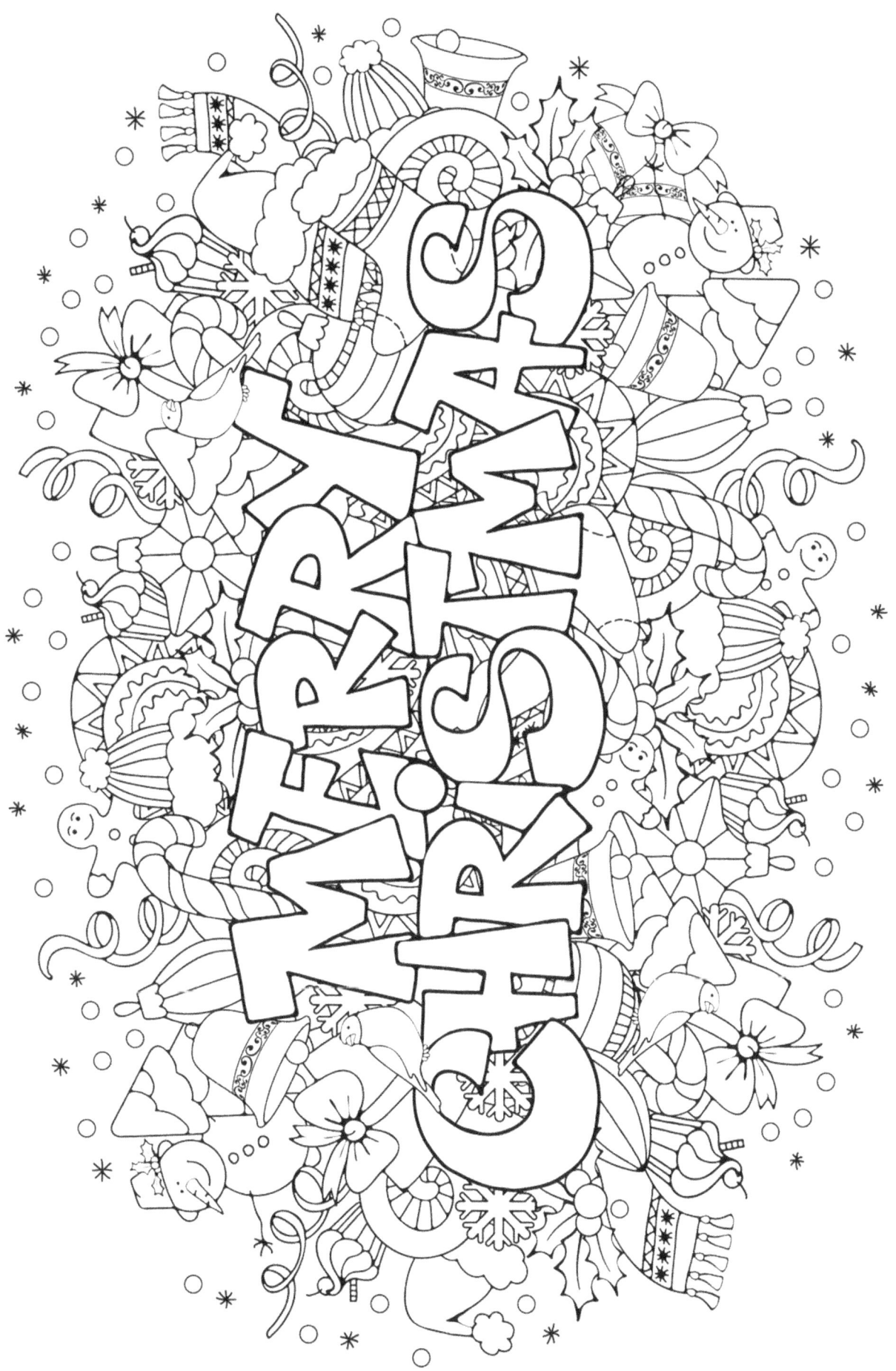